CONTENTS

FOREWORD

When Bishop Brendan Comiskey launched Fintan Tallon's last book, *Getting Down to Work – Creating Jobs in Your Community*, in 1993, he spoke in glowing terms of the author's work in promoting a community response to social deprivation and unemployment. The Bishop expressed his admiration for the excellent results achieved by Fintan in several programmes in Ireland, in particular in the innovative Tallaght programme undertaken for the Society of St Vincent de Paul.

My own reading of the book, and subsequent attendance at a talk given by Fintan, made me realise what a fresh approach he presented for Irish needs, drawing from his many years of experience in the United States and Canada developing community projects.

So, when we in The Limerick Enterprise Development Partnership faced the task of providing a realistic alternative to the crushing unemployment created by the closure of the Krups factory, I moved immediately to seek Fintan's expert advice. LEDP's mission statement owes much to his experiences, which he shared freely with our group.

In this new book, Fintan Tallon addresses the validity of his previous thesis to the current Irish "Tiger" economy and provides a deep insight into the widening gap between rich and poor in today's Ireland.

He presents a unique vision of how our national wealth can be used to benefit all of the children of the nation while simultaneously developing the nation's ability to face the challenges that undoubtedly lie in the future. His is a vision – one that can be used by urban and rural communities throughout our nation – of a new hope of restoring local economies, revitalising our ghost towns and villages, providing a greater sense of permanence to our rural communities and eliminating involuntary migration or emigration.

In this, Fintan challenges all of the people of Ireland to take the shaping of their destiny into their own hands. Certainly, in Limerick, we are facing up to that challenge.

Michael Tiernan
Chairman, Limerick Enterprise Development Partnership

Section 1

THE NEED FOR COMMUNITY ENTERPRISE

The first section looks behind the scenes of Ireland's economic miracle to expose some of the hidden problems. Many of these have to do with the death of community, as we become more self-centred in our lives. Community enterprise, not centrally-imposed solutions, can restore dignity and opportunity to our by-passed minorities.

Chapter 1

THE NEW CAMELOT

In Ireland today, belief in God is an optional extra — the real heresy is to doubt the existence of the Tiger Economy.

I belong to the Irish version of what the South Koreans call the "Generation of Sacrifice", who came of age in the late 1950s when Sean Lemass, Taoiseach of the day, preached the gospel of the rising tide that raised all boats and his economic guru, Ken Whitaker, introduced a programme that would eliminate emigration, unemployment and poverty within a decade. We were asked to sacrifice immediate benefit so that our children could get the education needed to ensure they had the knowledge and skills to achieve the New Ireland.

Now we have attained that dream. We have a booming economy integrated with the best economies of Europe. The Euro has replaced the Irish Punt. Official figures show that revenue returns to the State exceeded by £1.7 billion the surplus predicted in the 1998 budget and the 1999 budget predicts a surplus of £1.6 billion. Signs of the Celtic Tiger abound.

It has never been easier to obtain credit. Offers of low interest credit are screened regularly on our televisions and appear, almost on a daily basis, in our post. We are invited to buy a new car, take a luxury holiday, update our computers — in fact, achieve your dream today and pay tomorrow! The credit constraints of two decades are past and the curtain has risen on a time of general blessedness.

If the vision outlined by NCB Stockbrokers in a 1998 report is accepted, Ireland is on its way to becoming one of the "BMW economies" of Europe. NCB predicts that sustained growth in the size of population and in the number of people available for work will drive the economy forward. Irish economic growth will be up to 6% each year at a time when the ageing workforce will slow down the powerhouse economies of continental Europe. Subsequent forecasts have increased projected growth to 8%.

House prices are still rising, despite a 200% increase over the past four years. It has never been easier to obtain a mortgage and lenders, apparently, have few worries of a downturn in property values. Interest rates are lower and mortgages cost less.

Employment in the building and construction industry continues to rise by 11% year on year. Brickies, electricians and plasterers in the booming building sector have seen their weekly earnings jump by £200 plus per week.

The tax burden has been reduced, "take home" spending power has been vastly increased, employment opportunities for many have widened and future prospects look good.

Luxury car sales and new vehicle registrations are at record highs. Speculative buying of property to rent was once the domain of the few. Now a new breed is targeting this area to accumulate his or her own fortune. And the equity investor is obtaining record rewards.

Senior managers and directors in the private sector, convinced that the Tiger economy is of their making, are rewarding themselves well in excess of national wage programme limitations. More of them play golf on company accounts, use tax breaks to build large holiday homes and boost their incomes with Lotto-size share and profits bonuses.

Many of today's politicians and economists argue that, by the early years of this new millennium, unemployment will be a strongly diminished factor and will probably consist only of those classified as unemployable. Some speak of the dream of full employment being an imminent reality.

We have a National Plan to spend £40 billion over seven years, predicated on the continuance of the Tiger Economy and the revenue that it will provide to the State although, at its launch, the verbal small print cautioned that its achievement was dependent on favourable economic factors continuing.

So, **are** there any clouds to mar this glorious economic sunlight? Is there any downside in this new Camelot?

IN THE TIGER'S SHADOW

Well, yes, there are some for whom the Tiger has not yet roared.

There are tens of thousands of employees, pensioners and Social Welfare recipients who view the Tiger from behind a window of frosted glass and feel a mixture of envy and exclusion.

There is a vast army of public sector workers for whom the Trade Union movement claims "payback time has come" — clearly they too feel excluded.

There are countless thousands of our young, well-educated emigrants all over the globe who claim that my generation has given them everything but a future in their own country. Even if they could secure jobs in Ireland, the cost of housing alone would make relocation uneconomic in many cases.

There are thousands of the older generation, now retired on pensions, who find the value of their incomes eroded week by week and their standards of living diminishing.

There are the virtual ghost towns and villages of rural Ireland denuded by migration or emigration as local factories and shops close in the teeth of competition from multi-nationals.

There is uneven economic development, with most growth centred in Dublin and the East. Rural Ireland is discriminated against. In the West of Ireland, people say that the Tiger is afraid to get his feet wet by crossing the Shannon.

In virtually every one of our cities, there are ghettos that house the estimated 228,800 persons on the Live Register, on Community Employment schemes or on short term "training programmes". Yet, in 1980, the late Jack Lynch, then Taoiseach, said:

A Taoiseach's place is out of office if unemployment
in Ireland ever reaches more than 100,000.

Today's unemployed see no hope in their futures and this yields
a growing harvest of crime, civil unrest, drug addiction, broken
marriages and suicide. Many of these are categorised as
unemployable — which they are, without targeted programmes
to help.

The Conference of Religious in Ireland (CORI) pleads for
equality for the by-passed and the need for a new vision for Irish
Society. The Pastoral Letter of the Irish Catholic Bishops'
Conference, *Prosperity with a Purpose*, contains the same message.

The largest charitable organisation in Ireland, The Society of
St. Vincent de Paul (SVP), is so concerned about current poverty
levels in both urban and rural areas that it has adopted a new
approach. Where previously SVP relied on quiet diplomacy and
persuasion to influence public policy, it now publicly challenges
the State, its statutory agencies and local authorities to meet their
responsibilities to eliminate the causes of poverty by creating
equal opportunities and by re-distributing the vast wealth in
Ireland. SVP bluntly states that it and other voluntary bodies are
presently trying to stem the flood of hardship in areas, such as
homelessness, carers and disability, which should be a primary
duty of any State that claims to believe in, and legislate for, a just
society.

However, the 1999 Budget carries very little conviction of a
government determined to tackle either the problem of uneven
development or of the two-tier society that now exists. It was
greeted with dismay by both CORI and SVP with, it has to be
said, major justification. Virtually all the measures towards
eliminating social exclusion these bodies had urged on
Government were ignored.

HOW DURABLE IS THE TIGER ECONOMY?

The Irish and EU Dimension

Let us accept that the Tiger Economy does exist. The question remains whether there are factors within our present national economy, within the European economy or within the global economy that we can reasonably foresee as a threat to our Camelot?

It is axiomatic that, if social unrest is permitted to grow, the existing balance within our society could be upset dramatically and its future adversely affected. Blindness to the by-passed in society has caused eminent voices, like that of Professor JK Galbraith, to warn that we ignore the poor of society at the risk of alienation again growing like a living cancer. In Ireland, we ignore at our peril the by-passed in the present Tiger economy.

The Irish Tiger is founded on the twin pillars of 10 years of social partnership and of EU funding that poured capital into Ireland at an unprecedented rate. The jury is out as to which of these twin pillars have had most effect in producing the present Tiger economy.

If social partnership, how realistically can we envisage continuance? If EU funding, we know this has a terminal date — so we must ask whether the use made of that funding has created a self-sufficiency that will ensure continued growth?

A very significant percentage of our foreign trade and employment is tied into hi-tech industries established in this country by multi-nationals that can take their footloose investment to wherever they choose. Many of these plants can be threatened, virtually overnight, by ever-accelerating technical developments, some of which are very likely to erode or eliminate the market for what, today, are deemed world-leading products.

In addition, all hi-tech industries are dependent on a buoyant world economy for survival. Any major cut-back in this sector has very serious consequences for employment in smaller businesses supplying goods or services to the hi-tech sector, or dependent on the cash flow generated by the salaries and wages derived from employment in it.

What happens when EU funding is severely diminished or ceases, as it must in an enlarged community? What happens when the full effects of GATT agreements impact our agriculture and industry? What happens when the lower-cost economies of Eastern Europe, by then in the EU, are more acceptable locations for the multi-nationals?

Since our entire economic planning is predicated on a continuing Tiger, operating as part of a glowingly prosperous Europe, we must ask how solid are the foundations of the European Union itself? How far is the concept of the European Union itself predicated on growth in the global economy? These are questions that remain largely unanswered in published forecasts.

On BBC2's *Newsnight* in November 1999, Professor Martin Feldstein of Harvard painted a very gloomy picture of an EU of 15 sovereign nations with a single Central Bank. He argued that the Euro itself will produce unemployment, it being a simple economic fact that what is right economically in one country is wrong in another. What happens, he asked, in one country or one region, if local recession, caused by shifting multi-national businesses, creates large-scale and unacceptably high unemployment? National government is stopped from taking any effective action. The people suffering may decide enough is enough and lobby to disengage or pull out of the Euro — under EU treaties this can not be done. Feldstein argues that this scenario is not a theoretical assumption but the inevitable and certain consequence of merging a group of economically-incompatible nations.

Note that Feldstein's views expressed are not those of an anti-EU zealot. He is one of North America's leading economists, an advisor to Congressional Boards and several US and foreign banking and industrial corporations and his writings are viewed internationally with respect.

One factor alone illustrates that there is some validity in Feldstein's thinking. The different states that comprise the United

States give a variety of tax exemptions and grants to encourage local growth and, in contrast to the EU, there is no Federal power to intervene. The central power of the EU is trying to force incompatible economies in Europe into a common straightjacket!

The Global Political and Economic Dimension
Both the Irish Celtic Tiger and the entire EU economy can be beneficially or adversely affected by global political and economic factors.

In May 1998, British and American ex-patriates frantically sought flights out of Indonesia after massive rioting, following the collapse of the "Asian Tiger" economies of the region. Yet those who now promote the Euro concept had stated, less than three years ago, that the future belonged to the Tiger economies of Asia.

Over a decade ago, Japan was headed for victory in the world economic stakes. An economy built on small businesses had become a global investor, as the skylines of the world were being purchased at astronomical prices. In Japan itself, property values escalated beyond the wildest dreams of speculators. The combination of an absence of credit restrictions and low interest rates saw vast sums borrowed and poured into the most ambitious of land and property developments. The US, alarmed at the strength of Japanese imports into the US, demanded that the value of the Yen against the Dollar be strengthened — when the Japanese government agreed, the Yen shot up in value. There appeared a genuine belief that Japan was insulated against world events. The few lone voices that voiced fear for the future were branded as treasonable. How could the collective wisdom and balanced judgement of both government and business be wrong, when everybody was enjoying the fruits of economic success?

Then, the bubble burst:

- Property values fell by over 70 per cent
- Two leading investment banks and three Japanese clearing banks went into liquidation

- Construction workers, who had enjoyed years of euphoric earnings were now on the streets unemployed
- Homelessness became a problem for the first time in decades and many relied on soup kitchens to sustain life
- Politicians, bank directors and leading business-people faced criminal charges for corruption and fraud
- Pension funds lost over 90% of their value.

On top of this, Japan faces the domino effect of the collapsing Asian economy. World Bank economists now talk of the need for painful restructuring in all of the Asian economies. It is inevitable that the poor and socially-disadvantaged will suffer most in any such transition.

Further, any significant erosion of the widespread US, European or Japanese investment in Asia would dramatically impact the major world economies. The US is deeply concerned that the inability of Japan to achieve sufficient growth to overcome its difficulties could give rise to a Yen devaluation, making Japanese exports into the US more competitive and affecting the US economy.

Another nightmare scenario is a Chinese devaluation that would impact 40% of the Japanese and Asian economies and create a downward spiral of unpredictable consequences.

The former USSR economies are clearly in a mess and dangerous, economically and politically, to all of Europe. Yet the Western powers are seeking to impose, as a condition of aid, change to western-style democratic politics and a free market economy. This is akin to seeking to enter the Nuclear Age with a Stone Age axe! The International Monetary Fund package for Russia, in fact, plunged that country into chaos!

There has been over 70 years of centralism in Russia, with 250 million diverse people governed from the top of a pyramid. They have no knowledge of the simplest mechanics of the democratic or the capitalist systems, local autonomy, market pricing, floating interest rates, joint stock companies or competitive agriculture. Most are afraid to handle or adapt them to their purpose. Where previously the majority shared a low standard of living, today they have large-scale unemployment, food shortages and the elimination of free health care. Understandably, they have come to believe that Western capitalism is to blame, which was the message conveyed by previous administrations! The only fruit of the collapse of communism that they can see is the rule of law in free-fall. Seventy years of Soviet history cannot be changed overnight.

The Communist dogmas were the cement that bound the USSR together in all of its diversities of race, history and traditional belief. The cement no longer holds. Individual republics demand separate identities. These republics, locked in conflict and ethnic cleansing on a massive scale, could see the Balkan and East Timor horrors of the 1990s pale into insignificance.

Given that Russia can exercise a veto in the United Nations, that body is largely impotent. Former UK Prime Minister, Ted Heath, has warned that, quite apart from the general public refusing to accept the high casualties involved, NATO intervention would create a terrifying prospect for international law and government.

Some Western observers have argued that the position is not dissimilar to that of Germany in the post-war period and point to the German economic miracle. This ignores the fact that West Germany was under the stewardship of the Western Powers for a long period after World War II. It received massive Marshall Aid from the United States and its entire judicial, political and economic structures were rebuilt under the directions of the occupying powers.

The USSR is a very different scene. The former USSR could put space stations into orbit but the majority of the people on the ground shared a common low standard of living, cared for by "big brother" from the cradle to the grave. A logical economic aim would be to encourage, with massive "Marshall Aid"-style support, co-operative and community-style development for which the communist system has laid some good foundations. This could be conditional on all of the republics participating in some new form of economic federation, formulated so as to respect the national and ethnic identities of the individual republics.

The collapse of the rule of law in Russia is much more than an internal problem. A tidal wave of corruption and crime is being exported by the Russian crime cartels, with huge potential danger to the peace and economic stability of the whole of Europe, but in particular to the proposed new entrants into the EU.

The cold war between the USSR and the West helped many fragile Third World economies in Africa to survive. East and West poured funds into these countries because of their perceived strategic importance in a future war. This tap has now been turned off, with disastrous consequences to both the economic and political structures of the countries involved. Some, now ravaged by tribal conflicts, are regarded simply as bandit countries, best ignored.

The economies of most countries in South America are now early candidates for monetary intensive care units. The effect, particularly on the US economy, is unpredictable.

A major proposal from the World Trade Organisation is that the Western world allow free entry, without tariff, of manufactured goods and products from all Third World countries. The basis of the WTO argument is that this will raise living standards in the Third World. Is the real purpose behind this proposal to enable multi-nationals to establish in Third World locations and gain free entry into developed markets? If so, the repatriation of profits to the multi-national's home base will militate against any significant benefit or gain to the Third World country.

Already questions are being asked as to whether the US market has peaked. Remember, the US dollar accounts for 83% of all world-wide transactions. One of the original aims of the integrated European currency was to create a second mega-currency to counteract this dominance.

In summary, there is an almost incestuous complexity in the relationships between the world economies. For this reason, economists familiar with these intricate linkages, at best, are predicting the world economy to grow less quickly or, at worst, to go into a downward spiral of recession. The EMU and the new wider EU partnership are being launched into uncertain economic seas. Events outside Europe's control could force the necessity for harsh economic decisions affecting all member states. Will the good of the whole EU prevail — will the people of Europe be willing to become a new generation of sacrifice? — or will states react to establish the primacy of their own national interests? The history of the past decade does not give credence to the peoples of Europe responding as a united continental people.

When we boast of a durable Tiger economy, we need to remember the very narrow base of that economy and its vulnerability to events outside our control.

Chapter 2

AUDITING "IRELAND, INC."

One of the first lessons I learned as a management consultant was to do a short "management audit" in the initial examination of any client company to identify the internal strengths and weaknesses of the company's structures and operations.

In the case of "Ireland Inc.", there are five structures or essential building blocks that require examination. These are the key elements that make social and economic policies acceptable to the people and capable of implementation in a democracy:

- The political, government and administrative structure

- The judicial system, to protect the people against invasion of their lives, property and privacy

- The religious institutions to which the people belong — these formulate the social philosophies that are acceptable

- The banking and financial services

- The broadcast and print media.

A nation is composed of people, living in community, with a broadly common national ethos and objective. The essence of democracy is the participation of people in making or influencing the decisions that affect their lives. The extent of democracy in any country must be gauged by the range of matters that fall to be decided within the community itself and the extent to which decision-making processes allow for the participation of the public and are sensitive to the wishes and feelings of the public. Small size and more intimate communities ought to provide opportunities for greater public participation in public affairs, and to make it easier for citizens to comprehend and identify with their government.

POLITICAL, GOVERNMENT & ADMINISTRATIVE STRUCTURE

The ability of a nation, particularly an island nation of the size of Ireland, to maximise its strengths and minimise its weaknesses depends, therefore, upon a political structure, government and administration in which the people have confidence and trust.

Let us examine this in the context of contemporary Irish life. How far has the succession of political scandals, tribunals and enquiries weakened confidence and trust? Have we reached that sordid point where the only stable currency is the politic lie? Are Irish politics run on opportunism of party politics and not on national interests? How valid is the prognosis of several leading political analysts that future elections will see more and more independent candidates elected and that these independents will hold the balance of power over minority governments? Regrettably, one would have to answer "Yes", if only a qualified Yes, to all of these questions.

Within the revolutionary leadership that won independence for Ireland, there was a wide diversity of vision as to the structure and character the new nation should adopt. The tragic civil war that followed independence scarred the growth of nationhood and created a political division that dominated debate in the first two decades after the Treaty. This, more than any other reason, prevented a deep-rooted review of the government and administrative structure we inherited from the British. The Westminster precedent was not necessarily either the only or best for a nation of our size and social mix.

Up to the early 1960s, the impact of the values of the countryman in Irish politics was considerable. For very many years prior to independence, we had a peasant society of small producers of land who, with the help of simple equipment and the labour of their families, produced mainly for their own consumption and the fulfilment of their duties to the holders of political and economic power. The family farm was the basic unit of peasant ownership, production, consumption and social life. The ties of family and the land gave rise to the distinguishing characteristics of peasant life and thought. This was a pre-industrialised social entity that carried into the contemporary life of our newly-freed nation, specific, different and older elements of social inter-relation, economics, policy and culture. These characteristics led to a great emphasis on the personal and local in politics, reflected in the selection of candidates for elections, in electoral behaviour and the role of the elected representative and their relationship with their constituency.

At local government level, Ireland inherited a system largely based on suffrage for the landed classes. We adapted the system to give it a wider voice.

Eventually, in 1940, we introduced control by professional management through the County Management Act. Local management had a much wider knowledge of their area than central government, a knowledge built on day-today contact and involvement. County managers had the incentive to build on the strengths of local communities and, probably, had better prospects of encouraging local development programmes than either the government or the semi-State sector, both of which lived at one remove from the regions. Once professional management was introduced into local government, it was reasonable to assume that the local authority structure would then be used to make the administration more accessible and responsive to local needs and aspirations. Instead, central government progressively reduced the powers of local government over the succeeding years. The local role was diminished to little more than a rubber stamp on central policy. The whole drift of policy was towards centralisation.

There developed a political system welfare-oriented, centralised, bureaucratic, tamed and controlled by competition among highly organised elites, and, in the perspective of the ordinary citizen, somewhat remote, distant and impersonal.

The politics of this democratic system are above all the politics of compromise, adjustment, negotiation, bargaining; a politics carried out among professional and quasi-professional leaders who constitute only a small part of the total citizen body; a politics that reflects a commitment to the virtues of pragmatism, moderation and incremental change; a politics that is un-ideological and even anti-ideologic.

This system, and its governing ethos, marginalises small, rural and local communities.

So, having first failed to use local administration as a means of bringing democracy down to grassroots level, the momentum of centralisation led in fact to a style of decision-making that became more and more removed from democratic control. In turn, this has led to a decline in parliament's ability to be an effective critic of policy and a constructive force in government. The British-style Cabinet government belittles the role of the elected representative. Policy is made and public affairs are decided by ministers and their civil service advisors after consultation with the spokespersons of organised groups appropriate to the matter under review. All of this is a long way from the people's elected representative or from the representative assembly. The contribution of the elected representative to the crucial stages of decision-making is peripheral. More importantly, a chasm is created between local communities and central government.

Clearly, our politicians do not appear to believe in the participation of the people in the making or influencing of decisions that affect their lives. For the politician, community empowerment is a very delicate subject.

Why, I wonder, are we surprised when all of this has led to the type of conduct that the several tribunals were needed to investigate?

In my view, from the very beginning of the State, we might usefully have considered a much stricter division of power between the legislature (Dáil and Senate), the administration (Government) and the judiciary (Courts of Law). The US and French models are worth study in this regard. For example, in the US, a directly elected President picks his/her cabinet of ministers from outside the elected assembly. In France, the government is also chosen from outside parliament although, because of the greater parliamentary power in the French system, government ministers must reflect the views of the majority parties rather than the ideology of the president.

There is a need for radical constitutional amendment to restore faith in government. For example, the division of powers should be more effectively constructed and operated by excluding Dáil deputies from government office, as is the case in most other EU countries. This would secure a true separation of the administrative arm of the state from the legislature. The Government so formed would be answerable to the legislature. If European and US precedent is a guide, we would see deputies crossing party lines to vote on issues and far greater attention paid to local communities' aspirations.

The record low turnouts in recent UK and Irish by-elections show a critical apathy and a disillusioned public where party politics are concerned. Clearly there is a need for serious restructuring in the field of politics and administration.

THE JUDICIAL SYSTEM

The judicial system is the primary bulwark in any democracy that guards citizens' rights.

Two thousand five hundred years ago, the Greeks sought the golden key to perfect justice. We know that a small, earnest group of young men in Athens, led by Plato, held intense discussions that endeavoured to define justice. Plato transcribed the discussion in a treatise on politics and morality entitled *The Republic*.

The argument that justice was the interest of the stronger was rejected. After long debate, justice was eventually defined as being the harmonious balance between all of the other virtues, for both the state and the individual. Socrates described the ideal Republic as embracing this system of harmonious balances, which manifests itself in the justice dispensed by the courts and the laws of the land. As we start this new millennium, how far has this Grecian dream of justice been adopted even in the so-called free world?

Anyone who searches for this dream in the ethos of our present judicial system will be disillusioned. They will be startled by the number, perhaps only a minority, occupying judicial positions who seem to see their jobs as a source of power, a stage for their own egos. They will be very largely angered by the inequality of the justice administered to the less fortunate of society as against that given to the wealthier groups.

Certainly, particularly in the lower courts, there are members of the judiciary who have both compassion and a sense of humour. To them, justice matters more than the letter of the law. Sadly, however, the overall administration of justice in our courts is a lottery. One Senior Counsel, who lectures in law, puts it succinctly:

> I am a servant of the law but justice is an illusion
> unless the Almighty keeps better accounts than He
> seems to ...

The Courts of Law can be a daunting experience for litigants and witnesses alike. In Ireland, we have inherited the British judicial system in which the court is a place of contest and disputation, arbitrated by a judge and, sometimes, a jury. Every court has something of the aspect of a theatre, becoming a stage where the personages act out the rituals of revelation, conflict and resolution.

Laws are an imperfect expression of human rights as founded on the laws of nature and moral justice. None are fixed, immutable or beyond dispute or interpretation. It is a body of traditions, precedents and ordinances. Theoretically, it is dedicated in principle, if not in fact, to the security of the citizen, the maintenance of public order and the dispensation of moral justice. Sometimes these ends accord with one another. More often they are in contradiction. Justice may be ill-served while order, in the form of the rule of law, is more securely maintained. Because the law is an instrument and not an end in itself, there is always a conflict of opinion to arrive at its true intent. Inevitably, continuing judicial interpretation changes the character of laws enacted by the legislature by what John Marshall, one of the greatest chief justices of the United States described as "judicial legislation". This can, and does, affect both public policy and individual human rights.

For all of these reasons, laws can never be a perfect instrument of justice. More often than not, the courts are faced with the dilemma of conforming the cold unreason of legality with truth and moral justice. We then try to create the illusion that justice can be done by mutual compromise, inside and out of the courts. The law is discredited, public order is weakened and rests on a very frail apparatus of enforcement. This is why we seem to have accepted criminality in high places rather than prove publicly that we are largely impotent against it. The end is a divorce between politics and morals and a gulf of understanding by the ordinary citizen of the judicial system.

You know that we have reached the depth of human existence when, as a nation, we have to lean on legal enquiries to sort out every innuendo and every step in our political life. The very nature and duration of a public enquiry makes it an improbable instrument of justice.

Public enquiries and the courts of law, as presently organised and structured, are largely incapable of delivering the Grecian dream of justice. We find that the law is a lot of words that everybody reads to suit themselves. The law is incapable of loving and it cannot force people to trust. The Courts are perceived, however erroneously, as elitist institutions that defend the state and big business against what many ordinary citizens regard as justifiable community protest.

If we embraced the Grecian dream of justice, as a society and a nation, we would have a more compassionate understanding of the human condition and the wisdom to see how many of its miseries are incurable in this imperfect life.

RELIGIOUS INSTITUTIONS

We need religious institutions that encourage and promote the necessary virtues of justice, integrity, love, protection of the individual, family and community in the light of Christian belief, which is, supposedly, the dominant religious belief of the people of Ireland.

How far has religious belief and the confidence of the people in religious leaders and structures been damaged in the recent past? How much of traditional spiritual values was the cement that held Irish society and community together?

The leader of the Irish Labour Party tells us that we are living in a "post-Catholic society". Does he really mean post-Christian? Certainly, in Ireland and elsewhere in the EU today, there are a great number of people who regard any creed as no more than a set of prejudices.

It is fashionable to blame this falling away from Christian belief on clerical scandals. Certainly, these caused pain, suffering and horror both to the victims and the laity. But the number of clergy involved is statistically relatively small so that it is difficult to believe that this factor, on its own, is the only or indeed the major causative reason. Surely, this would not wipe out the inspiring work of the religious in both education and medicine over the past century?

In Ireland, and elsewhere in Europe since the early 1960s, it has become the accepted sophisticated norm to blame religion for all forms of extreme conservative politics. Writers claimed that the Church used its position to frustrate political and social change.

Certainly, the Catholic church in Ireland, up to the mid-1970s, was highly conservative in the actions of the controlling hierarchy. So, also, were the other Christian churches in Ireland and elsewhere in Europe. In Ireland, the churches bore the marks of a settled rural-based culture that had changed remarkably little over the centuries. The measured pace of rural life gave a tone to the Church and its style of government. There did not appear to be any good reason why the old ways should not persist.

But the post-World War II world in which the churches served did change. Communities throughout the globe were torn apart by divisions of political dogma, the brutalities of ethnic conflict and the dubious morality of regional wars, selectively waged in the name of democracy. The sanctity of life was denied.

The churches, in Ireland and elsewhere, must shoulder some blame. They accepted a dichotomy that is, in fact, heretical — the separation of religious life from social life. There is, of course, only one life, human life in all of its aspects. Man is a creature of Divine origin and destiny. Every circumstance of his life comes within the ambience of Christian thinking. This is the essence of the Gospel message. It has been stated and restated by Popes and other church leaders. Yet, over the past few decades, it was at best only marginally accepted by the greater body of the official churches. It is this failure that has allowed the re-growth of the doctrine of "survival of the fittest", an abandonment of morality in politics and business and a denial of our Divine origin. We can hardly deny the existence of God and then expect Him to appear if our harvest fails!

Many priests, religious and Christian pastors of all denominations have argued that the voices of the Christian churches have been edited out of existence by an increasingly secular press and broadcast media. Should they need to be reminded of St. Paul's exhortation to Timothy, written almost 2,000 years ago, when the Church was struggling to establish herself in the midst of very powerful enemies and when preaching the Gospel risked martyrdom?

> Preach the Word: be instant in season, out of season;
> reprove, entreat, rebuke in all patience and doctrine.

Paul is speaking, not merely to Timothy, Bishop of Ephesus, but to pastors everywhere, then, now and always, counselling them in the supreme tactic of the Word. The aim must be to inculcate patriotism founded upon divine law, to help keep humankind alive to the light of their souls, the hope of heaven, the love of God. The doctrine must be preached, over and over again, until the Word prevails.

The Irish Bishops' Pastoral Letter, *Prosperity with a Purpose*, is a welcome affirmation of Christian values and, in my view, a true following of St. Paul's exhortation. Tragically, our media has very largely ignored it and there is very little indication of it having any impact on national policy decisions.

I am still an optimist. I believe that the Spirit, which is immanent in all humans of goodwill, is moving the people of God, even in what appears to be a post-Christian world. Change is coming and will come from the people of God working with the Spirit. Change prompted by the Spirit will ensure the survival of Christian faith and values into this new millennium.

In this context, the Christian churches can become a powerful and dynamic force in the restoration of community values and in the generation of community empowerment. There is still a strong parish structure, which has the capacity to keep the churches close to communities.

BANKING AND FINANCIAL INSTITUTIONS

We need banking and financial institutions in which the people can repose total confidence that their individual, family and community interests will be promoted and safeguarded. How far have recent events eroded the very necessary confidence? Regrettably, quite considerably.

Ireland's two leading banking groups emerged in the 1950s when bank mergers welded together a number of previously independent financial institutions. This created capitalistic institutions that wielded enormous power, capable of good or evil. Two smaller competing banks, largely based in the North, were later acquired by British and Australian interests.

The demise of independent, locally-controlled financial institutions saw also the loss of a tradition that had been sacred to those who previously exercised control. True, these institutions had to be operated profitably, but genuine service was not made subservient to profit. By and large, branch managers of a previous era succeeded by being counsellor to the customer with whom a strong bond was formed. The character of the client outweighed his collateral. The risk, once taken, would never be abrogated; the contract was never hedged by legal tricks; a handshake was as binding as a formal document. The manager championed his client's cause within the bank's hierarchy, even when a failed harvest of one kind or another put his ability to repay at some risk.

In the new era, banking became the purveyor of financial services, of which money-lending was part. To increase profits, many in business or in farming were encouraged to undertake high-risk borrowing. Failure brought foreclosure of farm, home or business and a local manager's voice carried little weight. The new rich and the tax-haveners were welcomed with an enthusiasm that would have offended the ethics of a previous banking generation. Evidence before the Dáil Committee on Public Accounts in the last months of 1999 showed that the search for ever greater profits brought widespread instances of disreputable practices, including dishonest charges to customer accounts and the selling of services that were not in the customer's best interest. Bank branches in areas blighted by emigration and unemployment were deemed uneconomic and were closed, adding further to the demise of community. In financial circles today, loyalty runs a poor second to practical self-interest.

Small wonder that, in the final years of the past millennium, judicial enquiries and Dáil committees elicited evidence of malpractice that has eroded confidence in the integrity of banking. Can the position be remedied? It can and it must. Whatever about the State requiring a new constitution, banking certainly requires a new legal charter to restore public confidence. Clearly, self-regulation has proved inadequate. This is one reason why the ordinary citizen sees credit unions as being closer to community ideals.

A STRONG PRINT AND BROADCAST MEDIA

We need a strong print and broadcast media that voices the nations joys and fears, mirror its peoples' dreams and advocates peoples' freedoms. To achieve this, it needs a much closer link to communities at all levels.

The flood of reportage on television, radio and, especially, in the printed media on scandals in Ireland, the US and the UK does not suggest a media that informs, educates and helps in the evolution of societal change for the benefit of all of our fellow-creatures. There has been a huge growth in horror stories, scandal and gossip. The good in all of our lives is buried. When was the last time that good news was NEWS? When was the last time any leader, political or religious, was held up to the public as good, honest, upright and deserving of support? Feed a constant diet of disillusion into the minds of people and they become cynical and indifferent.

No-one can suggest that the journalist should suppress evil happenings. However, a more truthful representation of life is demonstrated by a correct balance between good and evil. This is a standard still adhered to by many of our excellent provincial newspapers and some, at least, of our periodical magazines. There was a time when the critical question of the effect of any story on the human being concerned or on the general public was foremost in the minds of editors. There are occasions today when one must wonder whether national newspaper journalism has become a blood-sport.

I write because I care. It is possible, at a pinch, and provided we have a reasonable civil service back-up, to do without political leadership. We abandon, at our peril, a strong printed media that can voice our joys and fears, mirror our dreams and advocate our freedoms.

BUILDING BLOCKS

Deficits in these building blocks of society can, in time, be remedied by the nurturing, at local and regional level, of community values.

The US witnessed in 1967 unprecedented riots in 100 cities, in which hundreds were killed, thousands injured and an estimated $1 billion in property destroyed. The US was then a country divided by the Vietnam war conflict, where social constraints were weakened, charitable donation a matter of tax deduction advantage and religious belief a garment to be worn or discarded at will.

The riots caused a re-think of values, a programme that set about rebuilding community in the ghettos, Churches that reverted to their correct role in society, vast changes in local and state politics, banking and media — even the criminal courts were forced to abandon previously ill-disguised prejudices against minority offenders in favour of a more enlightened administration of justice.

The Christian churches were impelled to introduce counselling programmes in ghettos comprising largely of people who had no belief in anything save the need of the moment. Counselling nurtured community leaders and a new self-belief in people. Money was forthcoming from Federal, State and municipal sources and also from banking and industry. This may have been prompted more by an enlightened self-interest rather than a Christian ethic, although more and more people returned to the practice of faith as knowledge spread of the Christian churches' role in combating violence in the ghettos.

We do not have to wait for riots. If, through planned community effort, we set about tackling, initially, the by-passed of our society and the rebuilding of local economies, the domino effect will produce the necessary changes.

Chapter 3

THE DEATH OF COMMUNITY

We have the immediate problem of those in Irish society by-passed by the Tiger economy. This can only be addressed by the provision of both community empowerment and effective specialised counselling. The aim must be to regain, as far as is possible, control over local economies. These micro-economic measures will probably require financial support from government or EU but can only be implemented by communities who know their rights because they have learned how to right themselves. The Irish Government tacitly accepted this principle under the Programme for Economic and Social Progress adopted by the social partners in 1991.

Community empowerment was openly encouraged by the EU Commission; in several debates in the European Parliament, officials indicated that this was the only way of ensuring that the development policies had a broad level of community assent, trust and support. The Irish government, realising that substantial EU grants were available for a programme of community empowerment, sought funding from the EU to support the initiatives outlined in the PESP agreement. In its application for European funding to support community inspired employment initiatives, the government claimed:

> The purpose of the grant is to support local economic development initiatives, stimulate new economic activity and support for local community-based socio-economic development. In particular, the grant will aim to support and tap fully local

enterprise initiatives and to promote integrated
economic, social and community development of
local areas. It will aim to support the main forces of
local development by providing funds to develop
local leadership capacity where required.

One official in the European Commission, previously a colleague
of mine in the UK, told me that when he read the application he
was pleasantly surprised that the Irish government seemed, at
long last, willing to devolve real power from the centre to local
communities.

Why then did the Area Based Partnerships, set up under
PESP and funded by the EU, fail to deliver the genuine
community empowerment so badly needed?

It is said that a camel is a horse designed by a committee. A
community empowerment programme, designed and
implemented by a bureaucracy for whom the dependency
culture was a sacred creed, was bound to have similar design
distortions! The Irish government tried to convince the EU that it
supported community empowerment. It referred to eligible
bodies as the 12 area-based partnerships set up under PESP
programme, other local community bodies and, rather vaguely,
private promoters. The area partnerships set up were, in the
main, staffed by persons recruited or seconded from the State
agencies; the boards and sub-groups consisted of State agency
officers and persons selected by them, but defined as
"community representatives". One of the few exceptions of
which I am aware is the Paul Partnership in Limerick, upon
which I focus in a later chapter devoted to an exciting
development in that city.

The bulk of the first EU grants to the partnerships was
allocated to projects previously funded by State agencies; a large
part of the balance was absorbed in the creation of a new tier of
bureaucracy. Worse, the partnerships were made dependent on
external funding and direction for their activities. As one
employer representative observed, every grant was subject to the
criteria of "eligible action" and innovation was not encouraged.

Overriding all of this was the fact that the partnerships were perceived by the people of the communities served as yet another arm of government; in consequence, it perpetuated the dependency culture.

Compare this to genuine community empowerment, which re-awakens a local sense of identity and loyalty and rejects a dependency mentality whether on the State or the EU. Once the true spirit of community enterprise is unleashed, there are no boundaries set to what any community can achieve. As we will see in a later chapter, one of the first actions of any local community enterprise group is to carry out an audit of the resources in or available to the local economy.

Irish governments, since independence, have failed to carry out an audit of the strength and weaknesses of the Irish nation. An audit of this kind would have raised very serious questions as to the wisdom of placing our economic future in the hands of multi-nationals and abandoning virtually all of our embryonic developing native industries. This, in itself, is the major cause of our diminished rural communities, ghost villages and towns.

If parts of the budgets devoted to the various programmes for the expansion of our national economy had been used for such an audit, we would have gained a clearer understanding of how to go about developing the resources of our economy and found answers to questions such as:

- Are there basic weaknesses in the structure of Irish agriculture that make it virtually totally dependent on government or EU support?
- Why has it taken until the last years of the 20th century to assess our potential in horticulture, fishing. mariculture, food processing, forestry, etc?
- Is there room to focus on areas of processing a wider range of actual or potential natural assets for sale on international markets?

These are the kind of questions that any competent management audit of the Irish economy would seek to answer. However, such an audit would have required the knowledge, co-operation and active involvement of each local community. The chasm that our defective political structures have created between central government and local communities made such a co-operative approach virtually impossible.

Yet all of these are questions that will need to be revisited when local communities come together to empower themselves to recapture their own local economies.

The area partnerships are yet another example of the Irish practice of formulating development policies in isolation from the community, in an atmosphere reflecting political aspirations more than concrete realities. In turn, this emphasises the gap between central government and the local communities that arises from a major defect in our political structures previously discussed.

When I have described, during seminar lectures, the development of genuine community enterprise and empowerment in the USA, UK and Israel, I have been told this form of development is inappropriate to Ireland, as the limited results of the area based partnerships demonstrate. Flaws in the design of these bodies and the use of spurious "community" components are arguments that are delicate to political ears! Yet it is the establishment of these flawed bodies that has led both to a lack of urgency in our communities coming together to seek genuine empowerment and to a perpetuation of a dependency culture that is the death knell of genuine community.

The grave shortage of entrepreneurial talent, demonstrated by the overall results of the City/County Enterprise Boards' initiatives, is often quoted by politicians to defend the *status quo*. Have our political masters so quickly forgotten that the emphasis on supporting foreign industrial establishment in Ireland led to the vast majority of our entrepreneurial talent emigrating to the United States and Australia, where opportunities existed to develop their talents?

With genuine community empowerment in place, individual communities will be able to follow the Israeli example of head-hunting our own emigrants, of encouraging those with worthwhile business ventures to locate in areas that need regeneration, through substantial relocation soft loans or grants.

The advantage of tackling this problem now, within the Celtic Tiger, has downstream advantages. It is inevitable that more individual communities will be impacted by factory closures — the evidence is in our daily news. The only question is how many, and over what timeframe. Pilot programmes, tested and honed to combat existing problems, will provide an excellent and immediate lifebelt to avoid disaster.

Some politicians have criticised my proposals as insular and parochial in nature; we are, after all, an intrinsic part of Europe. I do not believe that the EU is the touchstone of our economic salvation. Even if the chilling storms of world economic decline are avoided, this will only have a marginal effect on the native Irish economy.

It is a political fiction that the EU will eliminate the cancer of unemployment and emigration. The surrender of our economic independence will not bring jobs to Ireland for our children and grandchildren. If the EU prospers at a higher rate than economists now expect, at best this will provide employment in Europe for our well-educated children and not jobs at home in our own country. In fact, the expansion of the EU will probably accelerate the closure of many businesses that presently provide employment in Ireland. Of course, emigration to elsewhere in Europe will be defined as migration since we are all Europeans! This new definition does little to rebuild communities or restore our dying towns and villages.

It is not axiomatic that we forget the dream of stemming the haemorrhage of our young by reducing involuntary emigration. A mixture of political and microeconomic action as discussed in succeeding chapters could dramatically reverse the situation. We do, of course, need to get past the atrophied reasoning that seems to have guided so many of our policies to-date.

WHY IMPOSED SOLUTIONS FAIL TO IMPACT

Robert Jungk, professor of economics at Berlin University, wrote:

> Initiatives inspired directly by the people are
> probably the laboratories in which the twenty-first
> century is and will be developed.

I would go one step further and say that the initiative must not
only come from the people, but must also be implemented by
them.

Professor Joe Lee has commented that, in Ireland:

> ... reliance on government rather than self-reliance
> has become so ingrained in the public psyche that it
> tends to be assumed that nobody can act unless
> government acts.

In this statement, I believe that Joe Lee has pinpointed the single,
most important element that has created the two-tier society of
our present Tiger economy.

From the time of the First Programmes for Economic
Expansion in the late 1950s, our politicians, bureaucrats and
economic gurus have seen all problems in macro-economic
terms. Native industries and businesses, operating within and
providing employment for communities in the towns and
villages of rural Ireland, were jettisoned in favour of foreign,
mainly multi-national, ventures, encouraged with substantial
grant aid and tax concessions. The policy was justified on the
basis that it helped to build Ireland's industrial base and reduce
the country's over-dependence on agriculture.

While this had its positive aspects, it also had its downside. It
led, for example, to the major part of our distribution and retail
sector being acquired by foreign investors. The subsequent
growth in the supermarket culture, which bought much of its
product from abroad, eventually diminished our native
production of food. For many years, Ireland had produced the
bulk of its own food needs and, particularly during the war
years, exported substantial quantities to the UK. Over time, that

situation has been reversed. Nowadays, our food imports are alarmingly high. Basic consumer goods that could be produced in Ireland — fruit, vegetables, leather goods, shoes and clothing — feature heavily in our import statistics.

As traditional native industries closed down, jobs were lost, principally in rural areas. At the same time as Irish industry declined, the numbers at work or seeking employment grew dramatically. There was massive migration to the cities or abroad, tearing the heart out of many of our towns and villages. Some older readers will remember the late John Healy, in a memorable series of articles in *The Irish Times*, desperately pleading for "somebody to call Stop".

Economic planners failed to recognise that Irish industries were operated and controlled by people with strong local roots who had, in general, made a commitment to their area. The motives of the foreign investor were far more self-interested. As the value of foreign enterprise grew to dominate economic thought, pride in being Irish was rapidly eroded. Respect for goods made in Ireland became diminished. The acquisition by foreign investors of the largest segment of our distribution industry and the dramatic growth in the supermarket culture caused little public outcry. Yet, overall, the new owners showed scant regard for Irish economic development, pursuing instead policies of "profit-dominated" importing of goods. When this policy played a primary role in forcing the closure of one native company after another, their apparent failure simply worked to justify the contemptuous attitude held towards Irish-based industry. The fact that some survived, despite the odds, owes more to the combined determination of owners and workers alike than to any pro-active encouragement offered by the State or its economic policies.

Multi-nationals now account for over 50% of manufacturing employment in Ireland. In the main, they import raw materials and export profits and management fees. Their exports foster the illusion of healthy trade balances, one barometer of the nation's health. Since the 1970s, four hi-tech industries — electronics, computers, instrument engineering and pharmaceuticals — have accounted for about half of Ireland's industrial output, though they employ barely one-fifth of its manufacturing workforce.

The foreign industries and businesses preferred to locate within easy reach of international airports. We saw a disproportionate growth of population in the East coast, particularly in the greater Dublin area, and to a lesser extent in Galway, Cork and Limerick.

In all of this, rural populations and families were decimated. As more and more of our younger generation moved to inhabit homes in housing estates within ever-growing cities, their children would no longer laugh and grow up in the encircling comfort of the communities that were largely abandoned. Parents were no longer at hand to baby-sit, child-mind, do school-runs, or nurse a sick child or grandchild. This has led to families that have largely become small, selfish cellules, exclusive and possessive. Children who marry or simply leave the nest set up independent republics. After this, meetings between parents and children, grandchildren and grandparents, are far too often an occasional social thing. The idea of the extended family, interdependent on each other, which was a major feature of tribal or community living, has been very largely lost.

Unlike the community or tribe, the modern society that has evolved has no common faith, no common past, and no single frame of reference that can contain the diverse hopes and fears of its people. We have a new civilisation where we have to insist on what we are, prove our identity and then dedicate all of it, or part of it, as the price of admission to the group. We must conform, as team persons, faculty persons, and company persons — in a group to which we mortgage our futures to its demands.

Most of the economic and social planners, whose visions have created this situation, will accept the position as outlined. Their defence is simply:

> It is an illusion to believe that we can go back to the parish pump, with its small self-contained nuclear communities. We are one world, mutually dependent upon complex trade patterns and the

> distribution of diminishing resources. We have to
> rationalise and control a multitude of variables. The
> human causalities are inevitable!

I profoundly disagree. All life cannot, and must not, be lived in solely macro-economic terms. The past illuminates the future. We are all inheritors. We can no more shed our past than we can slough off our skins. It is at community level, the micro-economic, that the real revolution of hearts and minds should have taken place and where revitalisation must now begin.

People are not just statistics. They are fellow human beings who require a self-belief and a hope in the future. The simple fact of need creates the imperative to action.

Chapter 4
REBUILDING COMMUNITIES

The community enterprise organisation is the nexus of the community's needs and potential. Its authority comes directly from a community that decides to act together to achieve its goals. To sustain interest and momentum in community-based initiatives, a number of elements are essential.

The first is educating local communities to the possibilities of their area and the processes necessary to develop a meaningful community programme. To do this successfully, a dynamic, almost missionary, approach is needed, and the people who establish the community enterprise initiative must supply this dynamic as an ongoing process throughout the early years of any initiative.

The second component is the careful selection and training of both trustees and community leaders to head up the effort. All of us are gifted with different talents and should be encouraged to put our different abilities to work for the benefit of the community. Whatever our role, the skills we offer should give no grounds whatever for a feeling of inferiority or superiority. Leadership roles, in particular, should be taken on as a burden, not assumed as an honour. The politics of power is fatal to this process — indeed, the achievement of Episcopalian and Lutheran groups in promoting social revitalisation in urban communities in the US points to the advantage of an altruistic or Christian influence.

The energy of this initiative must be organised in a structure that touches and influences the community at all levels. Initially, the organisation must be largely voluntary, headed by an executive selected by the members of the enterprise group. Working groups take on the task of local research, carrying out surveys of skills, resources and needs, and investigating finance, premises and other specific issues that must be addressed. Ultimately, the aim of these groups' work is to produce a comprehensive community plan based on their research, and the community enterprise group then decides on the best way to organise itself to begin the work of putting these aims into effect. This permanent organisation, the community enterprise group formed in the style of a company or friendly society, must then oversee the implementation of the plan.

In the present era when the Tiger economy has given increased government and local resources, strategies that can provide creative and practical solutions to local needs must be developed. If government needs to redefine its role, in turn the private sector, and communities in particular, need to look realistically at what they too can contribute. Clearly, they are not asked to deal with government public spending, or to generate new public spending programmes. The past decade or more has demonstrated very clearly that local deprivation and unemployment is not greatly impacted by throwing money at the problem. A more targeted approach is required than is possible from macro-economics. But the local community, including local enterprise, must be willing to commit money and effort to a programme of community development if it is to have any chance of success.

Experience in the US suggests that the key to unlock local initiative is the community enterprise approach, which has the unrivalled ability to harness the potential energy and vitality of a new kind of public/private sector partnership. In response to the racial riots of the 1960s, big business, municipalities, state governments and the churches were forced to re-evaluate where the profit-driven economy was leading their society. The concepts of big being better, of profit overriding the rights of human beings, of communities being irrelevant in the global scheme of business, all required a sharp rethink. From that rethink emerged a compromise which recognised that community stability was probably better served by small business units providing rewarding local employment than by big business and mobile capital. Thus communities, business, local and federal authorities, often with church groups acting as catalysts for or trustees of the development, co-operated in programmes designed to reclaim the local economy by developing small business and community venture initiatives. A degree of success was achieved in the places where it was tried and, however limited, the outcome clearly pointed the way to achieving a more stable community life. The real tragedy was, and is, that big business would only participate in community programmes when it saw its self-interest would also be served.

The purpose of this kind of partnership between communities, local authorities, semi-State bodies and the State itself, is to ensure that policy decisions are taken only after full consultation and are implemented so as to cause the minimum possible disruption to the lives of the people affected. In this way, the participants contribute to the benefit of the broader community while promoting their own individual or organisational interests. The State recognises this in its interaction with, and support of, large business and pressure groups. Substantial areas of community life also benefit from, and in certain instances require, partnership. Local economy, community services, the neighbourhood — each involves economic and political factors that are neither exclusively private nor wholly public.

There are many simple examples to illustrate this practice of real partnership:

- Over a decade ago when we suffered very heavy snowfalls, many residents' groups and community organisations took on the task of clearing snow from pathways and shopping forecourts so as to help the overloaded local authority services concentrate on clearing the roads

- Many community and voluntary groups at present engage in reclaiming re-usable resources from waste, organising their activities to ensure what is left for dumping is collated for easy handling by the waste disposal authorities
- Voluntary visits to the aged and infirm reduce the workload on an over-stretched Health Board community service
- There are many examples of third-level institutes, professional training bodies and churches providing Outreach or distance education programmes to remote communities that would otherwise be unable to enjoy such services
- In a planning case in a Dublin suburb, where a planned development offended local residents, the community group avoided confrontation by persuading the local authority to offer an exchange of sites so that the development could go ahead in an area where it found a greater welcome.

The practice of effective co-operation helps create a situation where different demands can be satisfied, whereas confrontation is destructive to all the parties concerned.

Many years ago, a dedicated Garda officer warned that unless there was a considerable increase in funding to fight drug-pushing, the drugs problem in Ireland would grow to epidemic proportions. Sadly, subsequent events have proved him right.

Are we to wait for the inevitable explosion of anger, which the ghettoisation of the marginalised and deprived will bring to our society, before the State wakes up to its responsibilities? In the December 1999 Budget, when the State had an unprecedented extra £1 billion to dispense, there was no money for social inclusion. This, despite the fact that we were told, during the debate that followed the 1999 Budget, that one-fifth of the people of our Celtic Tiger economy are living below the poverty line.

Despite our much vaunted Christianity, concern for the marginalised seems to be a low priority for a society that is too often self-centred, unconcerned with its neighbours' difficulty. What has happened to the idealism that motivated the founders of our nation? To cherish all the children of the nation was not, for them, merely a pious aspiration, but a real objective.

We have the resources to take effective action to produce equal opportunity in the present Celtic Tiger economy. By doing this through genuine community empowerment, we lay the foundations for both a fairer society and a more durable growth. A nation built on those foundations will have a better capacity to withstand the impact of future economic storms — whether from unanticipated plant closures in local regions or a downturn in the EU or the global economy.

The governments and politicians of the former Asian Tiger economies used the times of wealth to prostitute themselves for short-term political gain. Luxury tourist hotels and offices disguised the ghettos, the violation of human rights and the enslaved inhabitants. Society, and the nation state, was made hostage to unbridled economic gain for the few. We ignore that lesson at our peril. We have the means to act — let us do so while we can.

Section 2

PRINCIPLES OF COMMUNITY ENTERPRISE

This section sets out the principles that must be applied if community enterprise is to be successful. From an example of successful community enterprise in Tallaght, an outline of the steps required is given. Finally, advice on counselling — at the core of community enterprise — is given.

Chapter 5

GENUINE COMMUNITY INITIATIVE

In the main, the by-passed in the Celtic Tiger economy are communities in urban and rural areas where factory closures have given rise to long-term unemployment and social deprivation.

Some closures have been due to multi-nationals relocating in lower wage-cost economies and/or because of technological changes. The temporary publicity surrounding these closures resulted in the creation of State-sponsored Inter-Agency Task Forces. Less publicised are the hundreds of communities all over Ireland where the government's own economic policies have caused the devastation through unemployment of previously thriving local economies.

The key objectives of community enterprise are:

- To develop a community response to this deprivation and disadvantage

- To implement a revitalisation strategy for any given area.

There is no grand design or plan that will be effective in each and every community. Needs, habits, resources and aspirations vary quite dramatically from place to place. In one area, the dominant need may be to generate self-sustaining employment for those who have been displaced from jobs by company closures. In another area, where only the skeletons of communities now remain, the task may be to rebuild the community by recapturing the local economy and attracting back to sustainable jobs as many as possible of the sons and daughters who have been forced to migrate.

The task of repairing and strengthening the community economy so as to provide new job opportunities in a thriving environment and to promote long-term community development is not a simple one. The means, too, are both diverse and complex. Local knowledge, backed up by research, analysis and planning, is fundamental in choosing the best strategy.

Community enterprise cannot and does not happen by accident: the initiative must come from people in the community. Those who take the first step must gather a small group of other concerned people, and sit down to talk about their community and the direction it might take. They must attempt to visualise the realistic potential of their area in economic and social terms, a process which very often starts by recognising that there are problems which can destroy the community's future if not attended.

Some years ago, I was asked at a lecture I was giving to just such a group how I could see any small community being able to take effective action to turn the tide of regional and national events that affected their lives.

I asked the group to step outside the present for a moment and to imagine that a nuclear Armageddon had occurred, but that they had somehow survived. In this scenario, there would be no local or State structure to give them aid. Would they die without it?

I didn't think so. Necessity would force someone in the group to assume leadership and the group as a whole would work to ensure its own survival.

When the group had overcome its immediate problems, it would naturally seek out other survivors, first in the neighbouring areas, later in a wider region. But this would be of little use unless the group had organised itself to a point where it had something more than sympathy to offer to other survivors.

Of course, if the group believed it was strong enough, it could try to impose its dominance on other surviving communities. Having already suffered so terribly from the effects of man's inhumanity to man, I would hope that the group would reach out to its neighbours in peace and the spirit of love and charity.

But the group quickly understood that, in extreme situations, they could survive (undoubtedly would have to survive) without the State. In better circumstances, they could also survive without the State and take charge of their lives.

If we are honest, we — each and every one of us — can see a two-tier society developing in our society. Some are benefiting substantially from the Tiger economy; others face unemployment and social deprivation, the consequences of which — crime, drink and drug problems, marital breakdown and suicide — are spreading like a living cancer through all of our communities, destroying our hopes and dreams for ourselves and for our children.

Instead of asking what the amorphous "they" are doing about it (and, at this stage, we might agree that "they" are not doing enough, nor are they likely to do so of their own volition), we must ask, "What can I do? What can you do? What can we as a caring community do in search of a remedy?". We will find that there is no strength to do anything until we come together but, if we combine our collective resources, our skills and ideas and energy, we can create a synergy that can make real progress.

There are many examples of how effective such community action has been in other spheres of activity. Take, for example, the Tidy Towns competition. Organised by Bord Fáilte, the competition is a good example of the positive results that can flow from a genuine partnership between the State and local communities, as well as an excellent example of the power of local organisation and endeavour. While Bord Fáilte provided the incentive, thousands of local communities throughout the length and breadth of Ireland worked long hours in planning and implementing improvements to their environment. In all of these communities, the local people had to learn to understand the different components that went into creating a pleasant environment. The organisers, for their part, had to overcome apathy, to generate teamwork, to find and to promote a common vision of how the community might be, and to work to a plan that was, and was seen to be, achievable. There were many Doubting Thomases when this competition was first started, but anyone who has travelled around Ireland in the last 20 years or so cannot fail to recognise the change that has taken place in the appearance of our towns and villages.

The Tidy Towns competition shows that the ability to come together and co-operate at local level is still very much alive, despite the corroding influence of state paternalism. And this kind of community spirit is vital if we are to launch a successful offensive that will bring the benefits of the Tiger economy to the by-passed of our society.

Change is desperately needed if we are, as John F Kennedy said, to have any chance of writing history rather than merely reading it. Structural political change, too, is necessary, but government and central bureaucracy will always see problems in the context of a national or international canvas; the subtle detail within the picture is best seen at local level. As author Evelyn Waugh points out:

> In small communities, quantitative judgements do
> not apply; a single gesture to alleviate pain is
> enough reason to act.

Politicians will not be forced into the necessary structural change unless communities of people exert pressure on them to do so. Such pressure will have all the more authority if it comes from strong, assertive communities — communities that know their rights because they have worked to right themselves. To do this, local groups must learn the essential principles of community enterprise, and must understand the concept that lies behind community action and the strategy that will help to implement this concept successfully.

RESEARCH: THE FIRST STEP

The first objective is to recover control over our own lives by recovering control over our local economy. The farming community did this throughout Ireland in an earlier era by establishing co-operatives; others in towns, villages and cities used the credit union concept to restore some control over ordinary people's finances; still more demonstrate the effectiveness of co-operation in sport and cultural organisation. In all of these cases, a shared vision unlocked the dynamic of people's energy, and set it to work within the circle of community.

To build a common vision of how our locality might be developed, we need first to look at what we have and what we lack. The community enterprise group's work begins with research that draws a picture of the local economy in its entirety:

- It looks at how the community as a whole gains its income and how it spends it

- It examines the needs of the community with the aim of identifying how these needs can be met locally

- It gathers together a register of all the skills that the
  community possesses.

All of these economic elements are audited, and the information
gathered in a comprehensive bank of knowledge that helps the
enterprise group to see where it might begin to act so as to
influence the local situation to the advantage of the community.

If we learn to source our needs locally, to the maximum extent
that we can, then we have recovered control of the local
economy. Examples abound, if only because most localities
spend huge sums of money each year on goods purchased from
outside.

> When a community enterprise group carried out a
> rough "energy audit" in two Welsh parishes, it
> found that they were spending some £250,000 a year
> on "imported" energy.
>
> On the basis of this information, the group began to
> look for ways to reduce this outflow of spending.
> Soon they were investigating ideas to develop an
> insulation programme in the area.
>
> The idea very quickly became an employment-
> creating enterprise, and resulted in a quite dramatic
> saving to individual households and to the
> community as a whole. The group eventually won
> contracts to insulate local authority offices and
> housing in surrounding boroughs and councils.

A comprehensive community audit that covers the whole of the
community's income and expenditure usually will reveal that a
range of products and services, which are purchased outside the
community, could be provided locally. Essentially, this research
highlights how local spending supports, or fails to support, local,
regional or national jobs. It is often surprising how little aware
people are of what they buy.

> A north Dublin group, located in an area renowned
> for its vegetable-growing, was taken aback when its
> research found that almost all the produce in the
> local supermarkets was imported.

Regardless of its price tag, an imported product can be a very expensive buy if it contributes to local unemployment, diminishes one's earning power and causes one's community environment to deteriorate. Government cannot discriminate in favour of home-produced goods without offending EU regulations but, using our individual freedom of choice, we can and must discriminate — a "buy local" approach generates revenue that creates local employment.

While this research will help to show how spending can be redirected for local benefit, the community enterprise group can also carry out a specific "needs analysis". By talking to local people and getting them to talk to one another about services or products they feel they are lacking, the community can begin to identify common needs that may be met by a little local organisation and enterprise. This proposition can be difficult to pin down, but careful research will help the group make intelligent choices between the different and varied ideas that this discussion brings to light.

> In a housing estate in Dublin with a large
> population of young married people, one need that
> emerged in a group discussion was that couples
> found it difficult to take a holiday because they were
> caring for an elderly relative and felt anxious at
> leaving them alone.
>
> A group of nurses who lived locally responded, and
> set up a "short stay" residence which looked after
> the older folk for a couple of weeks or even just a
> few days at a time. The initiative provided local

work for the young women nurses and made a real
contribution to the quality of local people's lives.

There are ideas of all kinds latent in every community, and new
ideas for products or services can also be discovered by specific
research in established sources.

Money, ideas and products are important, but a community's
greatest asset is its people. What do you really know about the
people of your area?

If an enterprise group is to work for the community, it must
find out who they are, how many are employed or unemployed,
and it must record the kinds of skills and aptitudes that are
available locally. It must also find out how many local people
have left the area to migrate or emigrate, what were their skills
and aptitudes, had any developed entrepreneurial ability for
innovative businesses that could be attracted back to inject new
life into the community.

This survey registers the human resources of, or available to,
the community. Armed with this information, the enterprise
group have a register of the types of skills that could attract
inward investment to establish in the area.

The register:

• Identifies potential entrepreneurs for start-up businesses

• Provides the essential briefing material for effective
  negotiation with state, semi-State or EU agencies

• Becomes the basis for targeted job placement and a guide for
  retraining needs.

The information gathered by the enterprise group can also be
collated and published in a directory of local trades, services and
businesses for circulation to households.

When a community group begins this quite far-reaching
research, it is bound to meet responses that vary from
enthusiasm to suspicion. But the primary issue in community
enterprise is to explore what we, the people, can do to restore
control over our community's destiny. If people really want to

achieve something positive in their communities, they must begin to do it for themselves. If this is to happen, the community must come together, with the aim of developing to the full what are, after all, its own assets.

The enterprise group's research aims simply to discover these assets and weigh their value. It does not just count local income, nor reveal who owns what locally. Its purpose is to look all the time for opportunities for local enterprise, for new ideas and proposals, and it tries not just to measure the *status quo* but to open up options for the future.

The very process of encouraging people to put their heads together, to think about their livelihoods and the life of their locality, brings tremendous benefits in itself. People begin to think and talk about what they might do. Ideas that may have lain dormant for years are rekindled. Subtle changes make themselves felt, slowly perhaps, but surely. Choices are made in shops; the new home-owner discovers that quite nearby is a carpenter who makes surprisingly inexpensive furniture and a fabric shop that can run those curtains up in no time. The community's skills and talents, whatever they may be, are brought to life by being brought to people's attention. And an environment that welcomes initiative, even demands it, encourages more from its members.

SMALL BUSINESS SUPPORT

If good ideas and people are combined with adequate capital and management, wealth and job creation will follow. The aim of the community enterprise group is to bring together these ingredients in the community, and so begin a process that will lead to the starting and nurturing of new businesses and the expansion of existing ones.

The small business — whether a 15 to 20-person private firm, an eight-person co-operative or a single self-employed person — is the life-blood of any local economy. Small businesses play a vital role in rebuilding communities, and a local economy built on small businesses is better able to withstand fluctuations in the national and international economy. In the recent past, entire communities, in Ireland and elsewhere, have been devastated by the closure of one large enterprise that was the area's principal employer.

However, the failure rate of small businesses is also extremely high — reaching as high as 90% of start-ups. What is needed, then, is a network to support the small business economy. It is not too much to imagine that every locality might have a network to care for and nourish the local small business community; in turn, the small business community will help care for and nourish the locality.

All local economies must try to retain existing business, to facilitate new ones, to attract outside investment and to foster a climate that supports enterprise. By doing this work consciously and methodically, the community enterprise approach increases the likelihood of success. All the time, the objective is to create jobs for local residents and to give purpose and support to the re-training and placement of the unemployed.

The community enterprise group fosters employment initiatives by circulating information and ideas within the community, and it also supports people with ideas for business or self-employment either by providing professional business advice and counselling, or by helping people with ideas to find the information and services they need.

I have seen several locally-based initiatives, started with a group of six or eight people, which grew to encompass a programme that now provides seed capital and professional business advice for local entrepreneurs. Communities such as these, which were able to raise funds for enterprise initiatives, have had significant successes. A company nurtured in one such community went on to become a successful exporter to some of the leading retail outlets in Europe!

It is true that less fortunate communities have had to work hard to overcome their relative disadvantages. However, every enterprise group must raise what it can from the community itself, and set up a working group to investigate all other potential sources of finance. With funding at its disposal, the enterprise group may provide capital directly to the entrepreneur or unemployed person setting up in self-employment, though this is rarely done. More often, the group helps people to access capital from programmes such as City/County Enterprise Boards, LEADER, philanthropic bodies and trusts, State grant aid and other sources.

Employment and enterprise opportunities are also created by:

- Targeting ideas that provide local businesses with the ability to expand
- Encouraging new business start-ups
- Establishing businesses by forming community companies or co-operatives
- Engaging in joint ventures with people who have the ideas, skills and competence to establish self-employing or business initiatives.

SEPARATING COMMUNITY SUPPORT FROM COMMUNITY ENTERPRISE

One of the major reasons for the uneconomic development of community initiatives in Ireland and part of the UK is the failure to separate community support from community enterprise initiatives. This happens because, in Ireland and the UK, the same community group undertakes both of these tasks, simply because of the difficulty of organising two separate groups of volunteers in the initial stages of any community programme. In the US, many community support initiatives are undertaken by separate organisations, such as church or local social groups, who then liase with the largely professionally-organised community enterprise group.

Community support work is essential before any meaningful enterprise programme can be undertaken; it also continues, indefinitely, thereafter simply because the need for such support in all communities is an ongoing feature of community life. However, support initiatives cost money and will never provide an actual monetary return on the investment of time and resources. For that reason, it will require continuing subsidy, either from the state or voluntary donations.

Community enterprise provides a range of services to small or start-up businesses, including accommodation, professional advice, secretarial, telephone answering, fax, accounting, VAT & PRSI returns and such like support **on a profit basis** to the enterprise group; the cost is more affordable to the client because the services are shared with other businesses. The enterprise group is, itself, registered for VAT and is expected to make sufficient profit to cover all operating expenses, to amortise the initial investment in set-up costs and to provide a reserve for repair and renewal of premises and equipment. In some instances, costings are done on a basis that can provide some of the finance required for the ongoing community support programmes.

The two goals of community action — to revitalise the social fabric of the community and to create self-employment or job opportunities — are distinct, although the two strands link together to strengthen the community's social and economic base.

The problem arises when support is given precedence over enterprise and where accounting procedures do not adequately separate the two very distinct initiatives; this is always a difficulty when the same community enterprise group is operating both programmes. The problem can be solved usually by ensuring that each programme is managed and supervised by a separate individual and that budgets for each are separately set and separate accounting procedures are adopted.

A support programme includes job matching, placement and training, and personal counselling to help re-build the confidence of people whose lives have been ruined by long periods of unemployment. In this work, the community enterprise group also has a key role, as effective community co-operation provides the organisation and incentive to counter social deprivation by social action. The vision of people who come together to set up a community enterprise group, many of whom may be securely employed and not likely to benefit directly from the project, extends beyond the materialistic. Theirs is very often a vision of a community that cares about its members and uses its resources for their benefit.

This social or ethical philosophy is in no way detached from promoting enterprise initiatives so as to foster employment. The social and physical revival of a community plays a large part in promoting its economic development, through identifying and encouraging the skills found in the community and through improving its social and physical environment — all of which make the area more attractive in which to live, work and invest. The group can organise plans for environmental improvement, non-commercial employment schemes, leisure facilities and activities, and disadvantaged minority support initiatives. To develop the level of skills in the local population, the enterprise group can organise second-chance education or specific training programmes in co-operation with local schools or through outreach programmes. The community can raise funds for these social developments, but usually they require permanent subsidy and must be financed either by charitable donation or State funding.

This level of intervention in the community demands commitment, though no more than is given at present to sporting, cultural and political activities throughout the country. The work of community enterprise organisation can be undertaken by voluntary staff, using the skills of local people trained by participation in seminars or by hands-on experience.

Professional guidance helps to get things done more quickly and full or part-time workers, some of whom can be recruited through social employment schemes, can relieve the burden on community activists. In the US and Europe, great progress is achieved at community level because community development programmes are given grants-in-aid to pay for professional input in support of voluntary effort. In some cases, the

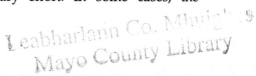

professional is expected to produce a blueprint of what can be achieved in the locality, which leads to wider local support for development plans. Professionally-developed community business plans are often essential if the community is to be considered for grants for building, training, technology transfer, etc. at a later stage.

In Ireland, when they are available, consultancy support grants are rarely adequate to cover the cost of employing professionals. The only other support on offer is the occasional appointment of a local enterprise worker at a salary scale that is derisory to the qualified professional. This lack of positive support has been a source of much frustration to community groups who have come together to organise initiatives in their localities. Their lack of experience, and lack of professional guidance, has caused many groups to concentrate on a narrow element of the community concept. As a result, they fail to develop the much broader programme of community enterprise that, in its scope and depth, builds a more solid foundation for future development.

Even so, local organisation, starting at amateur level, can do an immense amount of work and bring enormous benefit to the community, as has been the case in Tallaght and many other places where a local initiative has been tried. Yet, as the community enterprise organisation becomes an essential local institution, it will require at least some full-time paid staffing. Over time, volunteers will acquire confidence in their abilities, and the experience they have gained will in most cases qualify them to take on a professional role.

In contrast, the enterprise programme aims to promote the development of economic enterprise in the community, and does so on business-like terms. Though it may be put in place by the voluntary work of the enterprise group, the support service to business must be fully professional, either by employing a full-time business advisor or referring potential entrepreneurs to professional skills — legal, accounting, marketing, engineering, etc. — when they need them. The people who use these services pay for them, making the enterprise programme a self-sustaining project.

While the needs and the successes of each area will vary, within a few years of starting off, most communities will have tapped sufficient local enterprise to be in a position to establish an enterprise centre to house start-up businesses. Unlike the State, the community organisation should foster enterprise before housing it, rather than create an enterprise centre and then cast around for tenants. The enterprise centre should include a resource centre that offers regular counselling for actual or potential business ventures, and has access to legal, patenting, engineering and other relevant expertise.

DEVELOPING NATIONALLY

The community must build its own strength before it can look for, and make commitments to, other communities, business enterprises and organisations but, as community enterprise organisations grow, they will begin to contribute to regional and national development.

The community that has demonstrated its ability to manage itself and its ability to provide economic skills will be an attractive location for inward investment. At this stage, the community enterprise group can take on a more sophisticated role. Now it might undertake research:

- To assess the business developments that can be achieved in the area over the next three to 10 years
- To analyse the skills that will be needed to facilitate this development
- To set up training programmes to train people in these skills.

A project in East London, for example, attracted some sizeable entrepreneurs into the area by offering to provide them with precisely the categories and numbers of skilled workers they required.

The community group must also encourage large companies sited in or near the community to assist the development organisation.

> In one community in the UK, this liaison with local companies persuaded them to source goods and services locally, to second qualified personnel to assist the community enterprise organisation, to provide unused accommodation at favourable terms, and to put money into soft-loan funding for new business ventures.

Community enterprise groups can combine, nationally and internationally, to exchange ideas and information, and work with innovation, technology and business centres to access innovative ideas and new technologies.

Earlier, the energy audit undertaken in two parishes in Wales was mentioned. Energy options are only one area that benefit from a search for alternative ways of meeting human needs in a new and better way, due to the constant drain on non-renewable sources of energy. There is a great deal of interest world-wide in manufacturing fuel from organic sources, by turning the oil from plants or gas from sewage and waste into fuel. At present, the technology for converting these raw materials, researched in universities and other institutes, has been developed for trials in various locations. Many fuel products have already come on the market — in a French programme, buses are run on fuel processed from trees. New technologies create new opportunities — for example, in this case, the opportunity for farmers to use land that might otherwise be under-utilised (or set aside under the CAP) to grow crops for conversion into fuel. And while community enterprise groups will almost always start in a small way, looking at local needs in a local context, further down the line there is the potential to grasp such new and exciting innovations and become a part of their development.

Chapter 6
ACTION TALLAGHT

Shortly after returning from working abroad in 1989, I was approached by the Society of St. Vincent de Paul (SVP) with a request to carry out a brief survey of the south Dublin suburb of Tallaght and to present a plan for the area's revitalisation.

The area had been developed in the late 1960s and early 1970s on the basis of the "new town" planning precedent set in the UK and elsewhere. It was planned as a model town, where housing, shopping facilities, office complexes and industrial estates would all be constructed in a well-serviced and pleasant environment. In Tallaght, however, the concept went horribly wrong.

The planners had initiated a phased programme of first locating businesses and then building housing estates to accommodate the workers whom they would attract, but political priorities intervened. As a result, large housing estates were built before work was available for the tenants and, when businesses moved to Tallaght and brought their workforces with them, very little new employment was created in the area. The proposed landscaping and the provision of amenities also failed to materialise.

As a result, by the mid-1980s, Tallaght had become one of the worst unemployment blackspots in Ireland — indeed, in the European Community. In a community of 80,000 people, more than half were out of work and, in some parts of the area, unemployment reached 80% of the adult population.

Conversations with pastoral teams conveyed a sense of despair I had not encountered outside the most derelict inner city areas of the United States. It was difficult to reconcile this information with the Tallaght I had known many years previously, a pleasant rural village set against the backdrop of the Dublin mountains.

My first visits to this planners' "new town" left me drained and depressed. In one day alone, I counted 15 burnt-out houses. All around lay evidence of dereliction and disadvantage. The community lacked all but the most basic of services. Shops were protected with steel shuttering, fencing and iron bars as if to repel assault. Open spaces were here and there littered with burnt-out cars and rotting heaps of rubbish smouldering from recent fires. Rats scurried around the waste. It took me some time to realise that these rubbish-tips were the "park-land" spaces designated on the planners' maps as green zones or amenity areas.

The people seemed impotent in their dealings with a detached, uncaring bureaucracy. The sheer waste of government funding in spurious "make-work" programmes was evident — unemployed residents who lived in conditions of near squalor were put to work tending the gardens of schools and colleges. A social programme that used placebos to avoid confronting the real problems was matched by the amateurism of well-meaning but unskilled voluntary organisations. The anger I felt at these conditions turned to red-hot rage at the sight of well-guarded moneylenders holding Children's Allowance and Pension books as security on loans, forcing their debtors to surrender the cash.

Yet there was hope, too. In the badly-funded voluntary programmes for women and children, people were forging dreams of a better world. Many homes, neatly painted with well-kept gardens, stood like beacons in the midst of neglect. The courtesy and friendliness with which I was met in the homes I visited shone in stark contrast to their occupants' unending struggle against the twin evils of poverty and neglect.

I was convinced that the State could not provide a solution to Tallaght's problems. I was also convinced that, if SVP moved unwisely, it might be seen to assume the role of provider and it too would fail. But SVP, I felt, could act as a catalyst in promoting the idea of community empowerment, which would give rise to a community-level response to Tallaght's problems — that is, a programme initiated and controlled by the community itself.

My report for SVP was not what I had expected to write. Many of the remedies for social decay that I had seen in the United States were, for the present at least, inapplicable. The problems required a new approach, tailored to the circumstances on the ground. Even so, there could be no guarantee of success. At best, there was only a 50:50 chance of making a meaningful impact on the problems of the area. The alternative, however, was to surrender to despair.

TEN COMMUNITIES

On the surface, Tallaght seemed like one area, but I felt that in fact it was made up of 10 distinct communities, separated by strips of wasteland. Each had a similar identity of sorts, in part born of common adversity, but my visits had shown me that there were fundamental and basic differences. The error of the State agencies had been to treat Tallaght as a composite whole. In my view, the best hope of community revitalisation lay in adopting a more local approach, working with and building on this sense of identity in each area.

To start, we needed to find community leaders in each of the 10 separate communities. I was convinced that the potential for such leadership existed. Many Tallaght people had been wrenched from the city centre where they had grown up in closely-knit communities where families and neighbours had been important. Dispossessed as a result of urban renewal programmes and transported to an alien environment, they nonetheless brought with them a deep-seated and practical understanding of what community was all about.

The SVP's task force approached a number of local people, and over several weeks debated with them our view of how the Tallaght communities might begin to tackle the problems that surrounded them. These people were well aware of the problems, but needed to be convinced that a programme of self-help could make a real impact. In most cases, their doubts were overcome and they agreed to organise as a core group to initiate the project in each community.

THE LAUNCH MEETINGS

The core group's first step was to organise public meetings in each of these 10 locations. While the organisation of these meetings was the core group's task, because of their relative inexperience in matters of this kind, they needed a good deal of support from the SVP's task force.

Every adult in each parish was invited to the first set of meetings, which was held in schools, sports halls and churches. The objective was to discuss what response the community itself could make to the problem of unemployment. Introducing the theme, the senior member of the SVP laid out his organisation's desire to help in the work of revitalising Tallaght, but also set out clearly the limits of its role: to work in support of the community's efforts, but not to lead them. The absolutely non-political nature of the community enterprise programme was emphasised. The speeches were brief and to the point. I spoke for just 15 minutes, outlining what other communities I had worked with had done on their own account. Then I invited the audience to examine the self-help proposition in greater detail at a two-day seminar.

There was a big attendance at each of these early meetings. Many had come out of curiosity, some just to get out of the house for a few hours, and still more came with the energy and will to act. The question-and-answer sessions that followed the formal presentation were fast and furious as the people of the community catalogued the planning mistakes made in the area and the facilities which it lacked, and complained bitterly of how they seemed to be condemned to unemployment and a life of subsisting on social security. There were a good number of politicians from all parties present, and some officials from State agencies, and, when any tried to engage in speechifying, they were ruled out of order: the focus of the meeting was on the community and what they could do, not on what the political system would one day do for it. Not surprisingly, many of the politicians were none too pleased at the low profile they were asked to adopt, although some with whom I chatted afterwards agreed totally with the non-political approach adopted.

The people were hungry for new answers and, at the end of each meeting, over half the audience volunteered to participate in the community enterprise seminars. In the days and weeks that followed, the notion of "self-help" was talked about in the shops and homes and pubs of Tallaght and, in each area, fully 90% of those who had signed up for the seminar turned up on the day.

The SVP task force had requested that I should take on the role of course director for each seminar in all 10 districts, preparing the broad text of six 20-minute lectures each day, and working out a rota for delivery. Various members of the task force took on the job of finding suitable lecturers and worked with the local core groups to see that all the organisational details were carried out. Arrangements were made to find suitable premises, to organise tea and coffee and lunch facilities. A chairperson had to be selected for each seminar, and members of the core group briefed on how to handle the discussion groups that would follow each lecture.

THE SEMINAR

None of those attending the seminar knew quite what to expect — they were starting a journey into the unknown. To focus the discussion, I began by listing some examples of the way Tallaght worked as a community:

- A family who had lost its possessions in a fire had been offered an immense amount of support by their neighbours

- The people of one area had come together to undo the damage caused by flooding
- Another area had come together as a community to mourn the death of a child.

Outlining the main elements of a community enterprise programme, I pointed out that this work might well appear difficult or complex, but it was generated by community spirit such as they had shown, and could not succeed without it. If Tallaght's spirit could be directed into job creation, the community could not fail to benefit; the only question was to what degree.

Over the next two days, the community worked through an agenda that looked at the resources Tallaght might possess, the value of supporting the local economy, the importance of small businesses, and the structures of community enterprise organisation. Sitting in small "workshop groups", issues were debated in a way that allowed each individual to develop his or her understanding of the matters under review. As the seminar drew to a close, all the people who attended endorsed the initiative and selected an enlarged core group as a committee to monitor the progress of the entire programme.

AFTER THE SEMINARS

The months that followed the completion of the seminars were probably the most critical period of all. Follow-up meetings were held in presbyteries and classrooms as task groups were briefed and their work got underway. We had decided that, in the circumstances, a community audit would have little relevance and that, since the SVP had undertaken to find premises for the enterprise groups, a special premises group would not be necessary.

Instead, the emphasis was put on researching the skills available to Tallaght and building our understanding of the needs of the area, with a view to pinpointing how local people might begin to provide the products and services which were lacking in the community. Questionnaires were printed and prepared and the public relations group gave advance notification to all householders of the scope and extent of the questions. Teams were organised to carry out door-to-door research.

An early response in the local needs analysis showed that many members of the community wanted to see something done about the poor state of the "parkland" spaces. The community groups negotiated with the local authority and offered to help the County Council undertake the work if skips were provided. In a very short time, the vacant areas were cleared of rubbish and the Council agreed to begin landscaping and provide playground space for the children. For perhaps the very first time, a sense of partnership was generated between the Tallaght community and the local authority.

Over the next several months, there were many false starts, moments of near despair, and continual frustration at the slow pace of progress. All of the groups were trying to achieve too much too quickly, but gradually they were persuaded to hasten slowly, to take one step at a time.

Seven groups came through the first year, and grew in self-confidence and strength. Three fell by the wayside — curiously, these were situated in communities that would be regarded as the more affluent areas in Tallaght.

ESTABLISHING A PERMANENT PRESENCE

As the task groups continued with their work, it became apparent that, unless a permanent headquarters was found in each community, the entire programme would soon be in danger of collapse.

Fortunately, a retired local government official, an active and dynamic member of the SVP's task force, was able to use his contacts to persuade the County Council to allocate vacant premises to the community groups in four areas. In the other areas, unused church or school premises were licensed to the groups. The groups begged redundant office furniture from commercial enterprises in the local industrial estates and set about furnishing their new premises.

No funding was available from the State agencies. In fact, the community groups had to work hard to achieve even the simplest objective, like securing telephone and electricity connections. FÁS offered to finance the human resources and skills survey in one area but the offer was later withdrawn because of cutbacks in its budget.

The staffing of all community offices was covered by volunteers, who handled the queries that the public brought to them, recorded and filed survey results and monitored the activities of the survey teams. They brought a sound, common-sense approach to bear on matters as they arose, and only needed professional guidance to overcome unforeseen difficulties, such as when Social Welfare officers queried the unemployed status of people who spent so much time doing voluntary work for their communities.

BUSINESS AND EMPLOYMENT COUNSELLING

As soon as the community headquarters were operational, there was a surge of applications for business and unemployment counselling. This service was provided by SVP and was to play a major role in the success that was ultimately achieved in Tallaght. This aspect of community revitalisation and job creation is addressed in greater detail in later chapters.

The unique character of the service offered under this community programme became clear when, within six months of start up, people began to be referred to the programme by officers in the State agencies and by politicians in their constituency clinics.

Yet the programme was entirely dependent on funds that the communities raised themselves, and the subvention that SVP provided from its own very limited resources. Even today, State funding is minimal, and by and large does not extend beyond allowing the community groups to operate the Social Employment scheme which, in effect, replaces Social Welfare with an equal payment for 20 hours work on a community programme.

The lack of support was felt most acutely when the groups had to undertake both the human resources and skills survey and the local needs analysis out of their own resources. As the SVP's consultant to the programme, I was able to give professional assistance required in the drafting of questionnaires, instruction to the groups and the volunteers from local schools who undertook the field-work, and help in the subsequent evaluation of the survey's results. Carrying out the surveys effectively was a mammoth undertaking in such a densely populated area and proved to be a real strain on the programme's energy and resources.

This lack of State support is a cause of deep resentment to many of the community groups, particularly when the positive results of the Tallaght community enterprise initiative are there for all to see. Over 1,000 new business start-ups have emerged, with an estimated 70% success rate. Over 2,500 adults of all age groups have been assisted into full-time employment. A youth job placement programme was adopted. A very large percentage of the community were, when they first came for counselling, without hope or belief in themselves. They were written off by officialdom as failures and, sometimes, as unemployable. Yet, today, they walk tall in the dignity of either self-employment or in a job secured after acquiring new skills.

In the early days of the initiative, less than 10% of those employed in local businesses lived locally but, when the Square Shopping Centre opened, one of the largest complexes of its kind in Ireland, almost 60% of those recruited came from the enterprise communities' lists.

ACTION TALLAGHT

Membership of each community enterprise group is open to everyone who lives in the community.

The community groups are controlled by executive committees elected annually by the members, and represent their area more fully than any other comparable organisation has ever done. Because they are part of the community, the executive members are immediately conversant with, and reactive to, the daily problems of the people and of the area.

From the outset, I had hoped that the individual community groups would establish close relationships with one another as they matured. This happened and created a new dynamic — Action Tallaght, an association of all the surviving community groups. Because Action Tallaght is fully and truly representative of each community enterprise group, it derives its mandate directly from the people who live in the area, and is in a unique position to mobilise the resources of the community.

Today, Action Tallaght is accepted by the State and semi-State agencies working in Tallaght and works with them to secure a better future for all of the communities of the area. The role of the SVP, which initiated the community enterprise project, is now confined to provide counselling services as and when required.

The common objective remains community revitalisation and job creation. Many of those who came out of unemployment and succeeded in self-employment or employment used their new earning power to vacate local authority housing and secure new homes for themselves and their families. The majority of those now occupying these local authority homes bring the problem of unemployment with them. For them, the programme offers new hope.

New possibilities, new approaches and new ideas are continually opened up as the community's energy gains momentum. A whole series of programmes are underway that will lead in time to environmental improvement and to use being made of the natural scenic and leisure resources that lie in the nearby mountains. Youth programmes, and programmes to organise facilities and activities for the old, the infirm and the disabled are being organised, as are projects to encourage adult and second-chance education and affirmative action programmes to assist the most deprived within the community.

The long-term goal of the association is to achieve economic self-sufficiency. The top priority is to design and implement strategies to create jobs for the residents of this disadvantaged area. It is equally important, of course, to ensure that local residents are given access to the education and training needed to hold these jobs. It is interesting to note that, in some areas, where previously young adults rarely completed second-level education, many are increasingly progressing to third-level studies.

Action Tallaght adopts a comprehensive strategy that looks at the overall needs of the area, and tries to avoid the piecemeal approaches that were a feature of the past. This process entails the initiation, planning and management of innovative and holistic programmes. Achieving them will depend on the dedication, co-operation and commitment of the community groups, local businesses, state bodies, labour, educational and religious organisations. The human resources are in place; what is needed are the financial resources to employ the full range of professional skills to lift these projects to a new level.

The success of the Tallaght project could be increased several hundredfold if sufficient financial and other resources were available. By comparison with community enterprise programmes in other countries in Europe and North America, the present outcome has been achieved on a shoestring budget. The results owe much to a non-political approach and the fact that involving the community in determining its own future has generated a new sense of purpose, created a feeling of hope and sown the seeds of a new self-confidence in the community.

Chapter 7

COMMUNITY ENTERPRISE ORGANISATION

Many groups have been inspired to attempt the organisation of community enterprise projects. Too many have ended in failure; others have had some success, but fallen short of the aspirations of their founders. The reasons are manifold but, in my experience, the central cause has been that the structures set up lacked one or more of the essential building blocks of community enterprise organisation. Enthusiasm is no substitute for careful step-by-step planning — mistakes made at the outset will inevitably stunt subsequent development.

The Tallaght experience demonstrates how much can be achieved by people with minimal financial backing, initiating a project in an area with no readily-identifiable natural resources. Most places have a long tradition of community, institutions that work for the area's benefit, and natural assets that can be put to good use with a little skill and imagination. Many will also have problems of unemployment and/or emigration. Nonetheless, as the proverb says, it is better to light a candle than to curse the dark.

> In a Welsh community that faced significant redundancies when the local mine closed down, the community enterprise group approached the mine-owners and persuaded them to lease it to the locality rather than flood it as they had planned.

The mine was converted into a tourist attraction and is today the centrepiece of local tourism, drawing substantial spending into the area. Every day, hundreds of tour buses and thousands of cars bring visitors who, after viewing mine life on video and in the adjoining museum, go down the mine with miners' hats and experience for themselves the environment in which the miner worked.

Local slag heaps, slate and timber from mine-props provide the raw materials for innovative art and souvenir manufacture, tapes and books which tell of the mining history are produced and sold, as are replica miners' hats, lamps and tools. Local restaurants serve meals, including a wide variety of speciality Welsh dishes, all day long.

This Welsh community has found a new pride in being a Welsh mining town!

Tallaght had no mine, but it did have people who were willing to assume the enormous task of finding solutions to the problems that confronted the area.

The key lies in developing this community initiative in a way that makes it effective. In some cases, the community may be too small to develop an action programme on its own — communities such as these should find partners in the initiative. If it is to mobilise the level of skills and resources that are needed to create a successful project, a sustainable community enterprise initiative will usually need to encompass a group of communities and/or parishes over a wide geographical area. Bonding the people into an effective partnership may require the use of a branch structure, with each local branch requiring an active membership of perhaps 40 to 50 people to be self-sustaining. Its tasks include the setting up and operation of a local centre, as well as liaison with and represented on all the major activity groups.

The basic concept, structure and work of community enterprise is essentially the same, but its application will vary from place to place. The purpose, therefore, of this chapter is to illustrate the step-by-step approach required to translate the vision of a working community into reality.

STEP ONE

First, recognise that your community represents both a challenge and an opportunity. It is not simply a problem area to which there are no solutions.

People are the community's greatest asset. If migration or emigration has eroded this asset, the key challenge is to devise a programme that can redress this population drift. No matter how richly endowed with natural resources your area may be, they are still inanimate objects. Only people can generate ideas and initiative.

There are people who have inherited disadvantages and there are many who have been treated as outcasts by our society. For them, we must be prepared to reach outside tradition and precedent and construct affirmative action programmes that might include all kinds of uneconomic retraining — in literacy skills, for example, leading in time to second-chance education. The need for such programmes must be identified and planned by the community, with funding and/or outreach programmes sought from the relevant educational authority.

The majority, even on the margins of society, have latent abilities and skills that need to be carefully nurtured. Social research in the US revealed a higher level of entrepreneurial ability in the ghetto than in the more affluent areas, and I can confirm that much the same is true in Irish circumstances. I found more innovative ideas in Tallaght than in any other assignment I had undertaken. Given access to the necessary capital, people's own ability can provide job opportunities for people in the place where they live. The key lies in the realistic aspirations of the people in the community.

In the US Bible belt, there is a saying that all effective community action involves "visualising, prayerising and actualising". So, start with your own vision of what your community can achieve. Mobilise a small group of like-minded persons to share that vision. Now you have an *ad hoc* committee to organise a meeting of the full community.

STEP TWO: THE FIRST MEETING

The specific purpose of this meeting is to discuss and activate a community response to unemployment.

Every adult in the community should be invited. It is not advisable, at this stage, to expand the invitation list to include politicians and/or semi-State officials in their official capacity. However, if they are living in the community, they have an equality of interest with all other residents and should be invited in their personal capacity.

Too often, meetings on the subject of deprivation and unemployment turn into acrimonious arguments between the people, State officials and politicians. Since the primary purpose of this meeting is to determine what action your community can take, divisive discussion needs to be avoided. For this reason, the meeting requires a strong chairperson who can curb the possible excesses of fringe politicians or groups. A local school principal, or a leader from a women's community group, very often has the standing and local knowledge to undertake this task effectively.

The location of the meeting is a matter of judgement, based on the size of the community and the attendance anticipated. A local school hall may have adequate facilities — very often, a local church is ideal. The Gaelic title for a church was "teach an phobail", "the house of the people", and it is gratifying to see it revert to its traditional role in its use for important meetings of the people. I remember one meeting in Dublin, scheduled for the local Scout hall, that had to be transferred to the nearby parish church because the attendance exceeded the organisers' expectations by several hundred per cent. The most unusual venue I have experienced was a funeral parlour in the West of Ireland!

The meeting requires one or two speakers who can generate a new sense of purpose, create new hope and sow the seeds of a new self-belief within the community. There is no prospect in one short meeting of providing all, or even most, of the answers. The key lies in creating the hunger for answers that will come from the detailed research and analysis that comes later. For this, the community needs to be welded together into a team, its diverse abilities pursuing a common vision and objective.

The most efficient way of starting this process is to set up a one-day or, preferably, two-day seminar where, through lectures and workshops, an effective programme of community research will be developed. An agreement to set up a community enterprise group and to organise such a seminar is the desired outcome of the first meeting. If that is achieved, make sure to have the names and addresses of all residents who have agreed to participate.

STEP THREE: A SEMINAR AND WORKSHOP PROGRAMME

This is the foundation stone on which a successful community enterprise programme can be built. As such, it requires careful planning and resourcing. Very often, some or all of the cost will be borne by way of sponsorship by local firms.

The seminar must cover the concept of community enterprise, the geographic and organisational framework of the community, and look at deprivation and unemployment as both a challenge and opportunity.

In showing how the community will work to intervene in its local economy, the seminar will demonstrate how to organise a community audit and a human resource survey, and how to undertake a local needs analysis. The legal structure of the community enterprise group should be explored. The need to find premises for the group and to organise a permanent secretariat must be discussed, as will the community's ability to mobilise financial resources. Raising and using money demands that proper accounting procedures are maintained and this, too, must be looked at. The community must also develop clear communications and good public relations.

Experience suggests that this agenda is best covered in about 12 separate lectures over a two-day period. Maximum lecture time is about 25 minutes, and lectures need to be interspersed with small workshop discussions to allow for an evenness of understanding amongst all participants. Then there are coffee breaks and a lunch break each day. A final round-up decision meeting is held at the end of day two.

Retaining the service of a professional experienced in the subject matter as course director and lecturer is essential. Normally, the course director will recruit about two other speakers, so that there is a variation in voice, pace and delivery, though it is not unusual for all of the lectures to be prepared by the course director who then works out a suitable rota for delivery. Professionals with suitable experience can be found in the engineering, economics, business studies and legal faculties of third-level institutes or colleges, or in professional bodies.

It is vital, however, that the lecturer addresses the subject at hand — that is, the goals of community self-help. The purpose of the seminar is not to deliver the prevailing theory of economics or business or community politics, nor to inform the audience about State grants, training programmes or European funding. Lectures will touch on these topics, which are useful to the work of the community enterprise group, but their fundamental purpose at all times is to address the question: "What can this community do to help its area develop?"

Professionals with experience in community enterprise are rare in Ireland, though the debate on community initiative and empowerment has raised the profile of this issue, and universities and other institutes have responded by offering classes in community studies to the communities outside their portals. It is also essential to recruit the most experienced people from the community group set up at the public meeting to act as facilitators for workshop group discussions.

Choice of location for the seminar is crucial. It must be easily accessible for those wishing to attend, have an adequate auditorium or lecture hall to house the numbers comfortably, provide a sufficient number of smaller rooms for workshops of up to 12 people, a canteen for coffee breaks and for lunch, and adequate toilet facilities. In addition, if the community has a substantial young married population, it is desirable to organise a crèche for infants and young children. Normally, a local community college or school provides the best answer to these requirements, although weekends are usually the only time when these schools are available.

Before the seminar and workshop programme concludes the following require decision:

- Choosing a central or core group to assume executive control of the community enterprise initiative, to monitor the work of the group — particularly the research undertaken by the working groups — and to prepare a comprehensive business plan for the entire community enterprise programme. If a community support programme is also adopted, this requires separate planning. Generally, experience has shown that a programme of community support is put on the back burner until the enterprise group has gained confidence from establishing the enterprise programme

- Choosing a series of small working groups (each made up of four to six people) who will organise the work of undertaking the community audit and human resource surveys, and the local needs analysis, which are the building blocks of the community group's intervention. Further tasks that must be carried out include locating premises, arranging legal structuring, researching the full range of State and EU support programmes available to the community, mobilising financial resources, and organising inter-group communications and public relations

- Organising a temporary central secretariat to provide backing to the core group and working groups
- Setting a date, not more than one month later, for a full community meeting to receive up-dated reports from each activity group. A detailed time schedule is set out for achieving each task. Progress is then measured against this schedule.

Every person who undertakes to perform a role in any of the foregoing must be required to sign a confidentiality guarantee that legally commits them to retain in absolute confidence all information accessed during their work on the programme. This is a legal commitment, the breach of which has serious consequences. However, it is vital if the groups are to obtain the required information from members of the community at large.

STEP FOUR: GUIDANCE FOR WORKING GROUPS

Organising a Community Audit

As explained earlier, this broad audit of the community's income and expenditure is undertaken to find out the degree to which local spending support or fails to support local/regional /national jobs. Its aim is to discover where money is leaving the area unnecessarily, and seeks to identify when needs can be met locally. It deals with total community income and spending so as to build up a picture of the local economy — it is not concerned with how any one household either makes its money or spends it.

Even so, the very nature of the audit creates its own difficulty. Many people may regard a such comprehensive questionnaire as an invasion of their privacy. This objection can be partly overcome by designing the survey so that each household's response is conveyed anonymously.

It can also be argued, with some justification, that a random sample survey would provide a great deal of the basic information required. However, a key secondary objective of the survey is to focus the minds of each and every community resident on the positive or negative role that their personal everyday spending has on local, regional or national jobs. This is best achieved by a census of the entire community. Thus, this activity group should arrange the delivery of a questionnaire into every home, with a stamped addressed envelope to facilitate response.

The precise nature of the questionnaire will differ from community to community and will be influenced by sociological, geographic and other factors. In all cases, however, information is sought on total household income and expenditure:

- How much income is derived from outside the area — regionally, nationally or from abroad?
- How much comes from goods or service sold in or outside the area?

The objective is to get the best possible estimate of total cash inflows into the community.

Expenditure will cover items such as light, power, heat, rent, purchased services, household goods, clothing and food — the entire range of human needs bought and paid for by residents. In the case of power and fuel, the degree to which the presence or absence of adequate insulation increases or decreases the cost needs to be ascertained. This can provide both a useful business opportunity and a means of reducing the flow of money that leaves the community. The source of service and goods, in terms of point of purchase and origin, is relevant to the information required from each household.

A different questionnaire is required for local businesses. However, the objective is the same — that is, to determine where money is leaving the community unnecessarily.

It is desirable that this group should have, as a minimum, some professional guidance in the preparation of the survey and in the analysis of results. A community may well find that it has these skills in the locality, in the presence of residents who work in research or marketing.

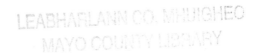

Correctly planned and implemented, this community audit can play a vital role in regaining community control over the local economy. The results can also beneficially influence inter-community support, and the exchange of goods and services between communities.

Human Resources and Skills Survey

In the past, many community groups have been persuaded to undertake this survey solely to produce statistical data and a report. This is not the objective. However interesting this result may be to state agencies or sociologists, it has very limited relevance to the planning of an effective community enterprise programme. The objective of this survey is to produce a precise, up-to-date register of the community that is subsequently used to target employment opportunities. It will indicate:

- Those unemployed, their age, sex, skill, experience and qualification level

- Those in this category who wish to explore the option of self-employment

- Those retired, their willingness to assist the community project and the skills they can bring to it

- Those currently employed, their willingness to assist and skills levels

- Those currently employed, anticipating redundancy, identified by age, sex, skills, experience and qualification level

- Those self-employed, offering products or service, who by inclusion in an effective community business and services directory could expand the volume of their business and create local job opportunities

- Those currently in second or third-level education, and the number of years until they will seek employment, as well as their anticipated qualifications and/or skills achievement.

All information sought during this survey must be covered by a confidentiality guarantee. The information is strictly for the community register and must not be divulged to third parties without consent. While every resident should be willing to supply the information required, if only from enlightened self-interest, there can be no compulsion. It is important that a negative response be accepted with courtesy and good humour.

Once this survey has been completed, the community has measured its most important asset. The information gathered forms the basis for action over a number of areas:

- It identifies potential entrepreneurs for start-up businesses
- It enables a detailed skills register to be put in place as a basis for targeted job placement, negotiations with potential businesses (attracted as inward investment), and as a guide to potential training or retraining needs
- It provides the essential briefing material for effective negotiations with State, semi-State and EU agencies
- It provides the basis for a realistic search for innovation and technology transfer.

Depending on the size of the community, the time and resources required to undertake this survey can be formidable. Professional help in the design, supervision and interpretation of the survey is desirable, though not essential if sufficient initial basic training is provided during and immediately following the seminar.

In the past, communities have received assistance from local businesses in the design and printing of the questionnaire and in the provision of computer facilities for processing the response. The people required for the heavy volume of field-work in many instances have come from senior students of local second-level or third-level colleges. In other cases, a Social Employment scheme has provided the necessary number of people required. However recruited, all field workers require basic training and hands-on supervision.

In addition, it is essential for adequate insurance cover to be in place throughout the survey. The human resource and skills working group must determine the most appropriate way of going about this work. However, the satisfactory conclusion of the work is crucial to the effective development of the community.

Local Needs Analysis

This is the area that causes most difficulty for community groups. The reason may be the catch-all nature of the brief and the inability of the group to see how a business opportunity can be developed from an apparently simple idea. The object of the analysis is to look at the needs of the community, to see how local people or firms can meet these needs by providing goods or services.

For a local needs analysis, in most communities, the most fruitful starting point is for each group member to organise a series of informal discussions held at random locations over the target area. Small discussion groups are best. A maximum number of 10 to 12 people is a good rule. A cup of tea or coffee helps to ensure informality. The working group members act as facilitators, encouraging an active discussion on what the group sees as community needs, and avoid promoting their own pet ideas. All ideas and information that come out of the discussion are noted.

> In an area in Northern Ireland, where a community group was looking at local needs, a considerable number of people spoke of their frustration in trying to clean domestic ovens.
>
> A young unemployed man latched on to the idea. He researched the best methods of cleaning ovens and then set up his own "oven cleaning round".
>
> Simple though the initial idea may have been, his enterprise has grown to a business with a six-figure turnover, employing five people.

In a similar example from the US, another young unemployed man got his business idea as he watched the underside of a pleasure boat being cleaned with a stand-alone pressure pump. He thought of the number of complaints he had overheard concerning the difficulty of cleaning oil and grass from shopping forecourts and domestic driveways.

Matching this information to the tools (or, if you like, technology) which were available, he hired the pressure-pump equipment and set about providing a fast, efficient cleaning service.

Today he employs 30 people, cleaning buildings, walls, industrial and shopping forecourts and domestic driveways.

It is all a case of meeting social needs at a profit. So let us commence with the basic concept that no idea is too simple to warrant consideration as a potential business opportunity.

As well as organising group discussions, a structured random sample research within the target area can also be productive. However, in my experience, most groups have found the result disappointing, probably because they lacked the technical expertise of professional market research organisations.

In addition, it is well to be mindful that the two activity groups previously discussed — the community audit and the human resources and skills survey — are already in the field drawing on people's time. Some groups have tried to add questions to these surveys as a method of targeting local needs analysis. The result was disappointing. It lessened the targeted impact of the other survey questionnaires and created a confused picture in the mind of recipients.

Product and service ideas, compatible with your community needs, can very often be discovered from discussion with appropriate divisions of Enterprise Ireland or the advertising pages of foreign newspapers and magazines. Other sources are the newsletters of foreign embassies' trade sections, US and UK enterprise agencies, newspapers and EU small business magazines. Local people now living abroad can be recruited as useful sources of intelligence, including obtaining directories of franchise organisations in foreign countries.

Next comes research among existing businesses within the target area to determine the potential for growth from the use of the ideas sourced.

When the community enterprise group has reached a stage of development that allows it access to innovative venture and technology transfer, this mechanism too can provide local existing business with expansion opportunities.

Close co-operation with, and a detailed study of, the results emerging from the human resources and skills survey is essential. This identifies potential entrepreneurs with business ideas, suitable candidates for entrepreneurial training and matching to compatible business ideas.

If this group approaches its tasks with an open, enquiring mind, free from prejudice, and avoids hasty judgement, it will significantly contribute to the community's revitalisation.

Premises

This is a specialist group with three central tasks.

The first is to identify and acquire an immediate, if temporary, base for the community enterprise programme. A group without a central operating office is handicapped from the very start. Its lack can cause premature failure of the community effort. Ideally, the premises acquired should be sufficient to house all the activity groups and be equipped to facilitate their smooth operation. Adequate security for confidential papers is essential, as is the arranging of adequate insurance cover.

Communities have met this first need in a variety of ways. In some areas, unused or under-utilised church or school premises were made available. In others, local authorities allocated premises for community use. Occasionally, private property owners were willing to licence the use of vacant premises, although this was occasionally frustrated by the loss of rates relief. Clearly, each community must seek its own solution from the properties available in the area.

The next task of the premises group is to determine, in conjunction with the other working groups, whether a centralised enterprise centre is required and whether, in say a widely spread rural community, a core centre with one or more satellite units is preferable. Much depends on what best suits the needs of the community and the circumstances that may have given rise to the initiation of the project.

For example, when a local plant closure puts out of work hundreds or thousands of workers, local communities cannot rely on "Big Brother" to provide a solution. The government may, and usually does, set up an Inter-Agency Task Force with a view to seeking a replacement industry. There is, and can be, no guarantee that this will be successful. However, if a strong local community enterprise group is quickly established, they can move to ensure that the site and buildings which housed the local plant are not sold and used for a purpose with a much lower employment quotient (or none at all).

Clearly, the community group should be examine the potential of acquiring and using the premises as an enterprise centre. However, unless the community has organised itself prior to the closure event, it faces a huge, uphill battle to get itself organised and the basic groundwork done — including the surveys discussed in previous steps — to be in a position to offer itself as a reasonable alternative to the closure.

An enterprise centre is only justified when there are sufficient small businesses looking for premises to make the provision of a centre viable. If a decision is taken to establish an enterprise centre, suitable premises must be found. Great care needs to be exercised in the choice of premises to minimise conversion and/or repair costs. It is also important to ensure that sub-letting through licences is not legally excluded.

The premises group will be responsible for the task of getting the premises up to the required standards for its projected use. This will require liaison with the planning authority, the local fire officer and familiarisation with departmental regulations. Thereafter, the premises must be furnished to the required standards with full provision of telephone, fax, power and light, security systems, etc.

In the medium to long-term, this group will assume the role of property managers for the community enterprise group. In relation to the enterprise centre, this may not be necessary if, as has happened in Europe, the US and more recently here in Ireland, premises vacated by a multi-national closure is acquired by a charitable company, set up by local interests, which makes available units to suitable locally-generated new businesses.

Legal Structuring of the Community Enterprise Group

Again, this is a specialist group that usually comprises lawyers and accountants who are resident in the community. However, unlike the premises group, this is an activity of limited duration.

In Britain and Ireland, the structure for community enterprise is usually either the Co-operative (or Friendly) Society or a Company Limited by Guarantee. Although personally I favour the second choice, it is really a matter of individual judgement. Since lawyers and accountants have both knowledge and experience of these structures, it is unnecessary to develop here the implications of the choice made. Both forms have an equally strong basis to encompass community enterprise objectives.

Regrettably, I have experienced many instances where unintentional omissions from the objectives clauses of the organisation have caused difficulties to communities at the later stages of development. Sometimes this can arise because of confusion as to the future activity of the community enterprise as it develops and matures. For this reason, it is best to outline the objectives which, in addition to the general objects usually incorporated, could beneficially be incorporated into the rules or memorandum of registration, whichever legal format is adopted. Accordingly, the objects of the Society (or Company) might be:

To undertake and perform all acts or deeds which the Society (Company) may legally undertake and perform which, in the opinion of the Management Committee (or Directors) will benefit the community of "X" and, specifically, but without prejudice to the generality of the foregoing:

i To make donations or subscriptions to any society, institution, trust, organisation or charity now existing or hereafter to exist for the general purpose of all or any of the following objectives — community revitalisation, the relief of poverty, the generation of employment, the provision of education and/or training in skills or otherwise for the betterment of individuals or communities.

ii. To establish and promote an enterprise centre, community support centres, craft centres, business and technology centres or workspace centres to encourage young people, unemployed persons and others to establish their own businesses and to assist small business enterprise.

iii. Contains the usual general clauses which give the Society (Company) the authority to acquire lands, property etc. and powers to borrow monies in order to promote the objects of the Society (Company).

iv. Empowers the Society (Company) to hire or supply labour for the carrying out of any work.

v. Provides that the Society (Company) may advance or lend any of the capital or other monies of the Society (Company) for the time being with or without security to persons, groups, societies or other organisations establishing business which in the opinion of the Management Committee

     (Directors) can generate employment or other benefits to the community.

vi   Empowers the Society (Company) to invest in and to take part in the management, supervision or control of business enterprises established for the benefit of communities and for that purpose to appoint and remunerate any directors, accountants, solicitors, business consultants or other experts or agents.

vii   To establish fundraising campaigns and/or promote, encourage and accept donations from any suitable source either in Ireland or elsewhere to provide funding which shall be applied to the objects of the Society (Company).

viii To promote surveys and studies to identify skills levels within communities and to identify and negotiate the transfer of compatible innovations or technologies which can generate employment within communities upon such terms and conditions as the Management Committee (Directors) in their absolute discretion may decide.

ix.   Generally to engage in any business or transaction which may seem to the Management Committee (Directors) directly or indirectly conducive to the promotion of employment or community revitalisation.

x.   To do all such things consistent with the laws governing the activities of Societies (Companies) as may to the Management Committee (Directors) in their uncontrolled discretion appear to be incidental or conducive to the purposes aforesaid or any of them.

The inclusion of these objectives should permit the Community Enterprise Society or Company to adopt and implement the most extensive of community revitalisation and job creation programmes.

Secretariat

A central secretariat has the task of co-ordinating and supervising the many activities of the community enterprise group.

Initially, it ensures that each activity group prepares and submits a detailed timed schedule for undertaking and completing its tasks. The secretariat will ensure that each activity group has, and maintains, adequate resourcing to achieve its objective, and tracks the progress of their work.

A secondary task of the secretariat is the organisation of security — for example, authorisation for, and the briefing of, all people calling on houses in the community, setting the limits of representation and the standards to be observed. Nothing should be left to chance. There have been too many instances of unscrupulous individuals fraudulently collecting monies from the public in the name of communities. Also the public image of the community enterprise group can be damaged by any wrongful act of any of its members purporting to represent the community, whether committed inadvertently or deliberately. The public should be actively encouraged to telephone the secretariat for confirmation of authority; local Gardaí should be informed of field-work taking place and the identity of the community field-workers. It takes only one or two careless incidents to destroy the most professionally-organised public relations programme.

The office of the secretariat will need to be open and competently manned during all of the hours when activity groups are engaged in field-work. This, in the early months, will require shift work operations and a programmed manning schedule. Staffing by just one person alone, either day or night, must be discouraged for security reasons.

The office of the secretariat will require a secure cabinet, adequate furnishing, lighting and heating, telephone, fax, a photocopier, a word-processor and all other normal office requisites. However voluntary, it must exude total professionalism.

Financial Resources Group

One of the most frequent of misjudgements of voluntary community enterprise groups is to regard this activity as that of a fund-raising committee. Its primary role is much larger and of major significance to the successful establishment and operation of the entire programme. Of course, like all other activity groups, its members must assist in raising the seed funding for the initial activities of the group. However, the financial group's essential task is to determine the budget needed to implement the overall enterprise strategy that the group adopts. It must liase with all other groups and anticipate their needs with accurately assessed cash-flow projections.

It is unlikely that any community will be in a position to raise, from its own resources, the whole or even the substantial part of the funding it requires. It is, however, essential that the community contributes to the extent that it can. A community unwilling to invest in its own development has no future. Consequently, all possible sources of community funding must be reviewed, including:

- Direct solicitation of funds from key business or private investors, who may be asked to give planned-giving investment over a three-year period

- The organisation of non-stop draws, social functions and other events.

There is a wide variety of state, local government and European programmes that can be used to leverage community funding. Some provide or pay for service or personnel costs, which reduces the burden on the community's own resources. Others directly grant-aid specific initiatives. There are a number of philanthropic trusts and organisations that give grants or soft loans in specific circumstances. All are sources that need exploring.

Central government funding includes direct grant aid from state departments which covers, among other things, recycling projects, community development, voluntary service to the deprived, and women's self help groups. Some local authorities provide grants in areas of extreme disadvantage for certain capital and development expenditures. The EU and Irish government semi-State bodies publish a wide range of literature on their programmes which requires (and often rewards) study.

However, caution is needed. Very many State programmes are under-funded and are subject to suspension without warning. This is one area where you do not count upon any receipts until you have a commitment in writing. Every community must keep its finger on the pulse of subvention programmes that may be beneficial in leveraging the community's own funding. Be aware, however, that the rhetoric does not always fit the reality!

To the financial resources group also falls the task of devising and introducing accounting procedures and financial controls. Where the funds of a community are concerned, things must not alone be right, they must be watertight. There must be no room for doubt. Nothing can damage a community more than the suspicion of malfeasance. The application of tight financial control procedures is not just desirable, it is essential.

Communications and Public Relations
The function of this activity group is to organise the flow of communication within the community enterprise group and between the group and the community.

Its work includes:

- Information flow between working groups
- Information to the broader community
- Liaison and co-operation with other national and international community groups
- Information releases to the general public and media
- Determining the best methods of obtaining accurate feedback of the general community response — essential if the community ethos is to be maintained.

Methods of communications are, at all times, a matter best left to
local judgement. They will probably include the use of a
community newsletter, church porch/pulpit publicity, public
relations releases to local and national press and radio, and to
television. This group should always be alert to human interest
stories that can focus favourable attention on the community
initiative.

More than any other, this group will determine the public
perception of the entire programme. To fulfil its function, it must
kept itself fully informed of developments within all of the
community activity groups. It must be an authoritative source of
information on the overall community enterprise strategy and
how it is being implemented.

These tasks present a formidable challenge, and demand a
great deal of discipline, dedication and effort from every sector
of the community. Yet work of equal difficulty has been
undertaken in many other spheres of life. Many of our
institutions — the agricultural co-operative societies, trade
unions, women's associations, sports and cultural organisations
— were built and continue to develop on co-operative
community endeavour.

In the same light, we can build a solid economic foundation in
our communities. If enough communities accept the challenge,
we will mine the full potential of our people, and help ensure
that national policies are framed to complement the work of
community enterprise initiative.

Chapter 8

THE MODERN ENTERPRISE COMMUNITY

Over a decade ago, I was part of a delegation seeking support from the then Minister for Industry and Commerce for a community development in Dublin. As we began to explain the concept, the Minister remarked that he knew all about community enterprise. He had an enterprise project, he said, in his own constituency. I discovered later that he was referring to a drop-in centre for the unemployed.

Yet, just a few weeks previously, the Minister had received a report from the National Economic and Social Council on the Liège community enterprise project, which had been introduced and funded by the EU Commission. Based on the success of the Liège experiment, the Commission had recommended that member states should consider the implementation of similar enterprise programmes in their communities.

Government ministers, and other charged with developing our economic policies, need to look again at the potential of community enterprise. The employment-creating possibilities latent in community-based initiatives are well-proven and documented. We need, however, to revisit the whole question of population drift, where the surge in the populations of our major cities is mirrored by the decline in rural population. Is this really justifiable on either economic or sociological grounds? Has any environmental impact study been made that would justify turning acre after acre, square mile after square mile, of rich,

arable farmland on the east coast of Ireland into a concrete
jungle? What political or economic doctrine dictates that we
exclude economic and social development from our near-
deserted towns and villages? Experience in the United States,
and to a lesser extent in the UK, demonstrates that such areas can
be revitalised and restored by effective community enterprise
action. Surely this should be encouraged, with legislation where
required and necessary, by central government?

The simple concept of community enterprise is not new.
People have always found the need for co-operative community
effort in order to survive and develop. The modern enterprise
community, however, was born in the United States during the
recession of the 1960s and 1970s, as an instrument for job creation
through new business development. It started with the
recognition that the foundations for the wealth of the modern US
business were laid during the depression of the 1920s. Over 60%
of the US *Fortune 500* list had grown from ventures started back
then by people with ideas like Alexander Graham Bell, Henry
Ford and Tom Watson. In the 1920s these people with inventions
and innovations, with different ways of doing something better,
worked for long hours alone in dark garages and old basements.
They became North America's entrepreneurs, providing goods
and services, creating jobs, building companies that grew and
made the free enterprise system work.

William C. Norris, founder and former chairman of the
Control Data Corporation, was one such businessman. He was
proud of the fact that he had clawed his way to the top during
the 1920s and 1930s as an entrepreneur. He had empathy with
the lonely innovator and, in the prosperous 1950s, condemned
the "shrine of big business" in a lecture at Harvard University.
Norris wanted to provide entrepreneurs and small businesses,
both servicing and manufacturing, with the same facilities and
support that large corporations enjoyed, without taking away
their independence. He planned to provide job opportunities and
a good working environment for depressed communities and,

above all, to provide a technology centre in which inventive ideas and individual initiative could grow.

Technology centres were founded to provide just such support for fledging businesses. And they proved successful: where the initial concept was adhered to, failure rates were reduced from 90% to 10% and wealth and job creation ensued. These successes were not confined to an educated middle class: very many inventors and innovators were from the black ghettos, some of whom could neither read or write. One black inventor who designed a small welding gun that revolutionised production lines and repair methods throughout the US signed his first licensing agreement with an X.

The demand for support for small business grew louder during the recession of the 1970s. One result of the recession was that the real importance of small business in terms of secure employment came to be acknowledged. Central to US initiatives, too, was the recognition that the 1980s and 1990s would prove to be a significant era for US industry and the growth of small business. As high technology industries such as electronics, telecommunications, data processing, energy and the biological sciences were beginning to burgeon and the service sector, including health care, advertising, banking, television, videos, etc. was growing to meet international demands, policy-makers saw that new business start-ups would flourish. Some might make the *Fortune 500* list for 2000 or later years, but not without outside support to dramatically reduce the average 90% failure rate of new business ventures.

As business and technology centres developed and flourished in the US, some of the leading third-level institutes found they were losing some of their most promising talent to these centres. They introduced an "on campus" variation of the theme under the title of innovation centres.

Thus, new expressions and words evolved in the US to describe the modern evolution of community enterprise and to denote specific kinds of approaches to supporting new business development. The terms "business and technology centre", "business innovation centre" and "enterprise centre" describe separate developments of the same concept, with differing emphasis on its specific aspects. The enterprise centre terminology came into use to describe the expansion of the technology centre concept to incorporate extensive social and community renewal, in addition to wealth and job creation projects. These terms have been borrowed in the UK and Ireland to describe very inadequate imitations of the original, and are used to cover everything from workspace developments to job creation programmes and advice centres.

The majority of these models do not adhere strictly to a given definition, because there is no universal panacea that can be applied to cover all the circumstances found in an area or community. Adaptations that draw on all models for inspiration are common. There is, however, one constant factor. This is the provision, at a cost affordable to all participants, of resource support, seed and venture capital funding and an effective system of innovative business and technology transfer — the licensing or franchising of business ideas developed elsewhere.

Wealth creation and job creation stem from meeting society's unmet needs at a profit, and many needs still exist. However, with very rare exceptions, entrepreneurs get the germ of their ideas from someone else. In addition, most innovators and inventors, whilst anxious to make money, do not relish the thought of corporate responsibility. So why not transfer ideas on a royalty basis? In sum, if you require an idea to start or expand a business, you can, most probably, acquire the idea on a fee and royalty basis from its inventor, whether it originates in the US, the UK or elsewhere.

Good ideas are available to small local businesses. Nonetheless, you can have the best idea since sliced bread but, if people won't buy it, you are wasting your time and money — at the end of the day, customer satisfaction is the key to successful business and secure employment.

In previous chapters, we have discussed what a community can do to support employment creation on its own initiative and with a minimum of professional help. Even on a shoestring budget, raised in the locality, the results will not be inconsiderable, as is shown by the Tallaght programme.

In many areas, whether rural or urban, the establishment of 15 to 20 small businesses and the placement of 50 or 60 people in employment will benefit the locality to an appreciable extent. And some communities can achieve a multiple of 10, 20 or 30 times these figures.

The community enterprise strategy, which has had such a marked effect in the US, and which has come to be recognised more and more in the European Union, is built on a number of factors. These factors, which ensure a several hundred-fold increase in the results that can be won by single communities, are:

- Expertise
- Financing
- Technology transfer
- Physical infrastructure.

Each of the elements is of equal weight and importance. The effective implementation of these measures demands an input from communities, acting individually and co-operating with other communities on a regional or national basis. It demands also the input of professional and industrial groups that can provide business expertise, of financial institutions, of employers' and workers' organisations and, not least, of central government, which must provide both financial incentives and enabling policies that will promote these vital measures.

THE EXPERTISE REQUIRED

The creation of jobs and the development of local economies is dependent on fostering the entrepreneur.

Generally, the entrepreneur is a lonely and often frightened specialist who is suspicious of those who offer him assistance. He is often unclear about, or unaware of, the assistance potentially available, or confused by the multiplicity of offers made to him — instead, he ploughs ahead on his own. He is usually undercapitalised, financially ignorant and familiar with only a limited number of management functions. His strength is his qualification and experience in his own speciality. When he decides to go into business, he is suddenly vulnerable, and this vulnerability is heightened by the need to divert his attention to unproductive day-today administrative activities. As a result, most potential entrepreneurs never succeed in creating actual businesses, and if they do, the likelihood of failure can reach 90%.

In the US and the UK, however, I have encountered very many different approaches that have successfully tackled these issues and reduced the failure rates of new businesses to about 10% of start-ups. Generally, this has been achieved by setting up consultative resource companies that provide services to municipalities, development authorities, local enterprise groups and individual entrepreneurs either on a fee basis or by way of equity participation in developments.

We have the range of expertise required for such resource companies: the suitable professional staff exist in third level institutes, industry, banking and in private practice. However, attempts made to set up such resource companies in Ireland have foundered.

This arises primarily from the common perception of the State as the grand provider. As a result, there is a deep-seated reluctance to pay for services that "the State ought to be providing".

Yet the success of the local community enterprise group will mirror the success of the small businesses developed by entrepreneurs. Usually, these are people who previously held a company job with a structured working life. Once they become businesspeople, however, their life ceases to have that structure. From the very start, they face choices that are wide and full of pitfalls and, all too often, they do not have the time, expertise or energy to cope. The entrepreneur, therefore, needs a business advisor, a champion who knows a great deal about organisation, operations, planning, marketing and financing. In no country in the Western world have I seen official State agencies with the resources and ability to fulfil this function.

Financial institutions and individuals will only invest money in seedling businesses if a return can be reasonably assured. Given the normal profile of the entrepreneur, this can usually only happen through continued monitoring of the young business by a qualified professional so as to ensure that the potential exhibited by the entrepreneurial ideas reach fruition. Professional assistance is vital if community enterprise groups are to establish working relationships and communications with similar groups and centres in the UK.

As a nation, and as a people, we need a fundamental change in our own attitudes. We need to abandon our huckster approach to life and realise the false economy of amateurism. If we are sick, we go to a qualified doctor; if our animals are ill, we call the veterinarian. If jobs are to be created, our local economies need a massive uplift in creative, productive activity. Surely, when our local economies are dying, even in our Tiger economy, and our children are facing the bleak future of involuntary emigration, we must have the sense to seek help. If the effort/reward ratio is right, the qualified professionals will be available to assist our development.

Financing Development

Webster's Dictionary defines venture as "an undertaking involving chance, risk or danger, especially a speculative business enterprise". Venture capital is the money made available for investment in such an enterprise. It is sought by a new or growing company to enable it to develop and carry forward its business plan, generally with an eye to the prospect of going public in the future. The capital is usually provided by sophisticated investors seeking speculative investments that offer potentially substantial capital gains.

A certain amount of capital can be raised in most localities for a small-scale fund, to be used to support self-employment ventures, the formation of a co-operative group or to help develop a small business idea. This can be expanded by using the financial support available for employment or business-related initiatives from State or EU funding. Valuable though this fund undoubtedly is locally, in a national context, given the geographical spread and numerical strength of those already by-passed by the Celtic Tiger, the scale of business development required can only be met by a national venture capital fund. The Culliton Report, produced in the early 1990s when the economy was still lurching from crisis to crisis, underlined the need for venture capital to be made available to small businesses. Culliton's plea fell on deaf ears.

If the Irish banks are to be persuaded to take an active role in this regard, it will require significant change in current legislation to allow them to do so. It will also require a sea-change in current thinking. Regrettably, in Ireland we have never had true venture capital companies. Those that have been established, usually with fairly substantial banking investment, have set minimum levels of turnover and market achievement that most businesses can only achieve after a considerable number of years.

This has left Irish entrepreneurs and small business dependent on bank borrowing, lease purchasing and hire purchase to finance start-up and initial growth. Seed and venture capital is not generally available and borrowing is usually subject to the provision of adequate security.

There is an indisputable need for small and medium-sized businesses to have easier access to capital for both start-ups and early expansion. The position in Ireland compares very unfavourably with that in other countries, like Germany, where a more active role is played by the banking institutions.

Israel achieved economic miracles with finance gained from Jewish communities throughout the world when it invited subscription to Israeli State bonds, with funds being invested in development projects in Israel. A bond issue backed by the State for venture capital investment in the development of Irish entrepreneurial activity would, in my view, raise considerable capital for investment both in Ireland and from the Irish abroad.

Capital raised in this fashion, coupled with an enterprise programme that contains the key elements previously described, could — and would — be a powerful antidote to the cancer of deprivation, unemployment and involuntary emigration that diminishes the live blood of our rural communities. Big ideas and small business go hand-in-hand but usually have more creativity than money. Properly capitalised, they have proven the most secure area for business and job development — in many areas of the US, 87% of all new jobs originate in small business.

The Physical Infrastructure
The community enterprise centre is the powerhouse of local development and requires careful thought at the planning stage.

Essentially, the centre offers small firms a place to work in an environment custom-built or adapted to cater for their needs. By co-operating with one another, the firms enjoy a scale of premises and facilities normally only available to larger companies. This is achieved by the use of joint service facilities, while retaining the intimate relationships and job satisfaction that come from working in a small firm.

It is in the area of physical infrastructure that communities or groups of communities can, even on their own account, play a substantial and meaningful role. Again though, these community efforts will require the type of partnership previously discussed. In addition, the task of developing this kind of infrastructure would be greatly facilitated if government acted by providing tax and other reliefs to developers or by releasing unused Enterprise Ireland space for this purpose.

There is no ideal type of building. In my experience, a very wide variety of facilities have worked well as enterprise centres — ranging from old stables and abandoned warehouses and factories to expensive purpose-built units or clusters. The simpler and cheaper the building the better, provided of course that it is consistent with the facilities required. Size is determined by a number of factors:

- The premises available — perhaps after a plant closure
- The cost of acquiring and converting them
- Local conditions and population.

The main criterion must be that each centre should show at least a small profit after having provided all necessary services.

Community enterprise centres are most successful when they are born from local initiative. In both the US and parts of the UK, there is a reluctance to support centres unless there has been strong local initiative in organising and financing them. Local communities must ensure that they are thoroughly involved either in establishing the centre or, where it is established by an outside body or trust, in doing the groundwork necessary to ensure that the centre maximises the impact on the local economy and employment.

When a community's work includes providing the minimum level of local funding, premises and land will attract support from outside agencies. There needs also to be local support for entrepreneurs by way of private funding, purchase of goods and service and finding suitable employees. At the same time, the facilities must be seen to be an integral part of the community — often achieved by using them for wider community needs.

Experience also illustrates that centres established without strong links to funding, management and consultancy back-up score minimal success.

We have already seen the dramatic results achieved by programmes in the US in the fostering of genuine innovation and entrepreneurship. Why has the same success not been achieved in the UK, where massive Government funding was invested, or in Ireland, where as previously shown significant EU grants were poured into the area-based partnerships?

It is true that the Irish and UK State agencies did copy some aspects of the US programmes. However, either they failed to understand or refused to accept the real innovative thinking involved. As a result, they perpetuated the dependency culture; where centres were established, they built up glorified workshops rather than true resource centres, and failure rates were and continue to be exceptionally high. The major reason is that virtually all of these agencies insisted on State ownership and control of both the groups and the centres.

A former US colleague of mine, in a report on the UK centres, stated:

> These institutes ... are not doing well because they are bureaucratically-oriented government institutions that could neither attract nor hold a real entrepreneur ... typically a guy who likes to take shortcuts, doesn't believe in paperwork, carries all of his ideas in his head, wants to make his own decisions ... he couldn't survive two weeks in State-controlled centres.

It is well to remember that a very large number of Irish emigrants, who were scorned for their visions in their homeland, found in the US centres a welcome and a culture that enabled their entrepreneurial skills blossom into success. Ireland's loss was an American community's gain!

We can create a society where the Tiger will roar for all. All that is required is the adoption of a more entrepreneurial approach that anticipates needs, identifies priorities and opportunities, and encourages an effective coalition of public, community and private efforts. We do not need to reinvent the wheel — the US models provide excellent precedents that can be followed with relatively little adaptation.

Chapter 9

COUNSELLING

The trauma that the racial riots of 1968 caused to society in the US saw the birth of a totally new concept — targeted counselling for the victims of social deprivation and unemployment. As was demonstrated on the SVP's Tallaght programme, this is a key weapon that must be introduced if we are to combat the levels of societal deprivation and unemployment which currently exist, side by side with the Celtic Tiger. It is needed both for its effect on our present problem areas and as a very necessary weapon in our armoury against an uncertain future.

I was first introduced into this specialised form of counselling over 35 years ago. I was then a consultant to a major US computer company that, with others, was spearheading programmes to combat unemployment and deprivation in some of the inner cities.

I approached the first talk that I attended with a large degree of scepticism. American society at that time seemed to have developed one form or another of counselling which, to some, merely helped people avoid the realities of life. I was to learn very quickly how misguided my preconceptions were. I began a journey that taught me many lessons in the application of skills to the benefit of others.

Seminar training followed the introductory talk. This was run by a group of counsellors who had spearheaded the massive effort to win back the hearts and minds of a suspicious, disillusioned people in the aftermath to the racial riots. They were a mixed group, coming from diverse backgrounds and religious beliefs. Many had been recruited by the Episcopalian, Lutheran, Anglican and Roman Catholic churches, which had devoted both material and human resources in attempting to find an alternative to violence. My initial expectation of Bible Belt zealotry was quickly dispelled.

The very first lecture set the scene. We were asked, individually and collectively, to confront the whole baggage of inherited belief, education and prejudices within us. These, it was pointed out, created an envelope of unquestioned certainty. We were challenged to face the reality that, while religion could provide solace and comfort for every human ill, it did not provide a cure.

The lecturers spoke movingly of their own first entrance into the coal-face of community indifference and intolerance. Within these deprived communities, they faced a total rejection of the assembly of believers because of their apparent certainties. To combat deprivation, the counsellors had the enormous task of overcoming the seemingly overwhelming odds of distrust, sometimes naked hatred and evil, while working constantly in an environment of enormous personal danger.

They went into the ghettos less than eight weeks after the racial riots. As believing Christians, most of the counsellors lived in a universe permeated by an immanent God with whom they could have a direct and personal relationship. Yet, the more they researched, the more they realised that the people they were endeavouring to help lacked belief in anything save the need of the moment. Virtually without exception, they suffered that real sickness of the mind which is the sickness of unknowing and uncertainty. They lived in that lonely world where all the gods were strange and there was not one to which the people could turn for hope or even the comfort of recognition. The counsellors had to find a method of bridging the gulf between their world and the lonely world of the ghetto.

Part of the answer came from the followers of Martin Luther King. He was preaching the impossible dream that prejudice could be overcome and that love was much stronger than hate.

The core of King's message was that every human being had to come to their God by their own road — that all Gods were but images of one and that which was done out of love must come from the source of all love.

They were shown how to abandon the arrogance of belief and how to realise that no two people come to happiness by the same road. From these thoughts emerged the concept of individual one-to-one counselling. Inherent in this was the abandonment of treating those living in the ghettos as groups or statistics. They needed to focus on the fact that each was a fellow human being sharing the same aspiration for a dignified place in human society. Trained to look behind the mask of individual despair, counsellors quickly found that the same Spirit is immanent with the same Divine attributes in each and every human being. Once that perception of unity was grasped, an unbearable chaos could be turned into hope of future restoration. The eventual societal rejuvenation achieved by these pioneering US counselling programmes testifies to their success.

In the months and years following that training seminar, I have been privileged to build on the lessons learned and to practice the skills acquired. Initially, this was in various parts of the US. For many years, and as long as the memories of the racial riots were fresh in the minds of politicians, substantial funding was made available both for training and operation of these programmes. Regrettably, the span of human memory of tragic events is very short. Within a space of a few years, political priorities were reordered, US society in general reverted to the selfish, insular attitudes of the era preceding the racial riots. Against this background, by the mid-1970s, most of the US counselling programmes ceased with the unavailability of trained counsellors.

Proof of the effectiveness of the early US counselling programmes was dramatically illustrated by the riots in Los Angeles that flashed on to our television screens in the early 1990s. These riots had erupted because of an attack on a black youth by a group of LA policemen. Previously, this would have spurred a domino effect of riots in a host of other city ghettos. Instead, in all of the cities that had introduced counselling following the earlier riots of 1968, the event was marked by peaceful protest. As the US breathed a collective sight of relief, few realised that the credit lay with those missionary counsellors of a previous era who had nurtured community leaders and small business developments within the ghettos. Los Angeles was one of the few cities that did not introduce counselling following the earlier riots. Instead, it preferred to throw money at the problem in the form of establishing a plant where a major US corporation provided production line employment.

THE FIRST PILOT PROGRAMMES IN THE UK & IRELAND

Shortly after returning from the United States, I was invited by former colleagues to assist in some community revitalisation programmes in the UK. Many of these programmes were funded from central government budgets, supplemented by grants from the local authorities, which in the UK had far greater powers than their Irish equivalents.

The thrust of most of these programmes centred upon encouraging outside investors to establish in areas of deprivation and/or to encourage local entrepreneurs, through business counselling, to establish businesses based on concepts that they had developed. In the task of encouraging outside investment, the different local government areas were in fierce competition with each other. There was a significant lack of suitable local entrepreneurs coming forward with worthwhile proposals. Many officials argued that it was not realistic to expect new job opportunities to emerge in disadvantaged urban or rural communities. They argued that resources were better employed in special education, training and community programmes of the people development variety. These were claimed to provide the necessary ingredients to qualify people to take new jobs when and wherever they arose. Migration from an area of disadvantage to a more prosperous one was accepted as the inevitable price of progress! The social consequences were ignored.

From my experience in the US, I was aware that this argument had to be viewed with a measure of caution. It relies on the premise that jobs, in the traditional sense, would eventually become available. It ignored the fact that technological changes have dramatically contracted employment opportunities in both manufacturing and service sectors. Recruitment to the public sector, to insurance, banking and other traditional white collar employment, in both Britain and Ireland, were either frozen or reduced to a fraction of previous demand. More and more white and blue collar posts were being changed into contracts for self-employment. Thus tanker drivers, carpenters, plumbers, electricians and delivery persons were joining the ranks of the self-employed.

Yet, realistically, despite these changes, long-term or permanent involuntary unemployment is neither inevitable nor economically justified. Wealth creation stems from meeting the unmet needs of society at a profit. The pattern of human needs changes and the constant challenge is to identify and transform those needs into business opportunities. Wealth and employment, whether nationally or locally, are created by putting together ideas, money and people to produce goods or services that will be bought and paid for. Creating a job for ourselves is no longer a task for some amorphous third party. It is a personal challenge to each and every individual. In most, but especially in deprived communities, personalised counselling is an essential tool to assist individuals face that challenge.

Persuading the bureaucracy in Britain to accept this fact proved difficult. There was an ingrained dependency culture which I found quite a shock after having operated so long in the free market economy of the US. Within the British dependency culture, the bureaucrats found it virtually impossible to accept that a successful entrepreneur could be nurtured through targeted counselling. It was my own experience, shared by some of my British colleagues who had also worked in the US counselling of the unemployed programmes, that once you remove the shackles of a dependency culture, once you encourage the human mind to reach out and assail the barriers that appear to strangle ambitions, a new dynamic is created. There is much unmined talent to be discovered in the most unlikely places, so many unfulfilled dreams waiting for their hour. In those dreams, our future begins. Not everybody has either the talent or the dream, but targeted professional counselling of a specific kind does help many people discover talents and dreams that had previously lain undiscovered in the darkest recesses of the mind.

Now, the bureaucrats were forced to accept, as a fact of life, the high failure rates in many local and regional economic development and job creation programmes throughout Britain or their failure to grow and significantly impact on social needs. To them, this merely demonstrated the lack of a general entrepreneurial culture amongst a significant proportion of the population. They were less convinced that reliance on proposals and ideas emerging from candidate entrepreneurs was, in itself, a major causative factor. My colleagues and I knew, from our US experience, that without the benefit of intensive counselling, these schemes were usually unproven and had a high mortality rate. This was also the experience on the European mainland.

My colleagues and I were eventually permitted to operate a number of pilot programmes in the UK. Subsequent research showed a 60-70% success rate in start-ups within the pilot schemes. Regrettably, the wider use of counselling in the UK programmes did not develop. A precedent-driven central and local bureaucracy was unable to allocate funding for the provision of counselling training. A number of programme managers who had participated in the pilot schemes found their plans to make counselling an integral part of revitalisation proposals stillborn.

When, in subsequent years, I was retained to assess the efficacy of a number of UK programmes, this emerged yet again as a serious factor. There was in most of the areas I surveyed a comparatively low number of suitable applicant entrepreneurs with the confidence, skills and ability to undertake the challenge that the new entrepreneurial culture presents. For far too many, self-employment was seen as a last resort in the fruitless search for employment; to others, it was perceived as a lonely, frightening marathon; and to some, it was merely a means to garner a hand-out until something better turned up. This raises the question whether an enterprise culture can ever flower in a political system that fosters the cult of dependency.

When serious illness forced me to abandon my nomadic business lifestyle for many months, I became involved in the SVP Tallaght programme discussed in **Chapter 6**. The communities of Tallaght at that stage faced similar problems to those faced in the American ghettos — a huge degree of impotence and helplessness existed. For this reason, one-to-one counselling was made the cornerstone of the SVP's programme, differentiating the Tallaght programme from any other programme for the unemployed anywhere else in Ireland either at the time or since.

Counselling in Tallaght was made available through the locally established community enterprise groups. Initially, the groups organised these sessions as if the people were attending a doctor's clinic but, when I found myself arriving a community house with up to 20 people at a time awaiting interviews, I quickly realised that this would not work. An appointment system was introduced so that each person could receive adequate assessment and counselling. In the early stages of the Tallaght programme, not all who came for counselling had the best motivation. Many came out of curiosity, others to claim their share of the cake, still more to demand their rights. The majority, however, had a basic idea for a business, however tentative or ill-formed. For many, this idea represented their paramount source of hope, and it was essential to tread softly to avoid trampling on their dreams.

After the basic soundness of their ideas were assessed, each person was shown how to test the viability of the project by doing some basic market research. They were shown how to determine the cost of accommodation, plant or equipment, and where to find these things. Finally, once the idea was shown to be feasible and marketable, they were assisted in preparing business plans and applications for funding from State agencies or voluntary trusts. Since the majority of applicants were unemployed and could not provide collateral, they were not regarded as good risks by the commercial banks.

Not unexpectedly, many ideas foundered at the initial stages but, even in these cases, the individuals involved felt that their effort had been worthwhile. They had carried out their own research and had proved or disproved the value of their ideas for themselves. At worst, the effort they put into these projects gave them new energy to explore other options open to them.

From over 1,000 counselling sessions in the first year, more than 100 people succeeded in starting a business. Some found a new outlet for the skills they had used when employed, others developed ideas from hobbies, and over the next three years their businesses showed a 75% success rate. The type and variety of start-up covered a wide range, including machine knitwear, educational toys, glassware, upholstery, signmaking and signwriting, shopfitting, joinery, printing, security grid manufacture, computer programming, food preparation, soft toy manufacture, craft work of all kinds, curtain manufacture, and specialised paint mixing. Services included sewing machine and domestic appliance repair, laundry and dry cleaning, furniture repair and reconditioning, and a whole range of building maintenance. These new self-employment ventures initially used the enterprise community's premises, which are a community resource and as a business address.

There were some very real technological innovations that went on to achieve outstanding success and, in later years, were recipients of very substantial EU grants for expansion. While these cannot be identified for reasons of confidentiality, the story of one is worth recording.

When I first met Tony he had been unemployed for over four years. A handsome man in his mid-30s, his demeanour conveyed an aura of despair when he first came for counselling under the enterprise programme. The recession in the shipping industry gave him little hope of re-employment in his former job as shipping engineer.

Tony had a product idea for which had tried to obtain support from a variety of State agencies, which he felt had rebuffed him with scant hearing. From his attitude, it was clear he had little faith in our meeting producing a different result. Indeed, he admitted that he had come largely because the local employment exchange was insisting that he undertake a job-search programme — this would teach him how to prepare a *curriculum vitae* for a job. A highly-trained individual, Tony regarded this as the last straw in his unequal struggle with bureaucracy.

He opened a cardboard box that contained the results of years of painstaking research, and began to explain his idea for a product to assist the disabled. His aura of despair disappeared as he described how it would work. Over the next few hours, my initial curiosity turned to admiration as it became clear that he had come up with what seemed to be a dramatic technical advance. If it could be shown to be economically viable, I was convinced that Tony's innovation was vastly superior to any comparable product available.

His prototype, however unimpressive in appearance, was an excellent example of inventive genius. Why, I wondered, had he received such a negative response from State agencies? I personally knew many of the officials to be intelligent, perceptive and compassionate. Had he failed to outline his ideas adequately? Perhaps that would explain why his concept was misunderstood and its potential unrecognised. After all, it had taken several hours of patient listening and questioning before I could formulate an opinion. Perhaps, pressure of time on State officials had prevented a similar appraisal.

Today, Tony's product is marketed in several countries. A number of leading US corporations acquired licences to produce it. The EU allocated substantial funding for research and development to widen the scope of the product's use.

An idea developed in the bedroom of a West Tallaght home brings comfort and joy to a multitude of disabled people around the world. Yet without the community enterprise programme, Tony would be yet another failed dreamer.

Could his product have been manufactured here in Ireland? Probably yes, but this would have required a much more flexible approach from our semi-State bodies to funding and a much more courageous venture capital approach from our financial institutions.

More importantly, Tony is not alone. There are scores of others, people with innovative ideas, with new and different ways of doing something better, who because of the programme today walk tall. All were unemployed, either through redundancy or lack of opportunity. They felt lost, or mourned their old, comfortable occupational patterns. The enterprise programme helped them overcome their anger and frustration, and helped them see that, rather than feel negative about the loss of what they knew, they had to find the courage to feel positive about what they could create. This is one of the key objectives of a successful community enterprise programme.

My single regret from the Tallaght programme is the fact that the most promising of the innovations which emerged during counselling had to be referred to foreign companies for ultimate development and manufacture. The entrepreneurs and inventors received benefit but their skills and the skills of hundreds of others throughout our country were lost to the nation of their birth.

Not all who came for counselling were suitable candidates for self-employment in the ideas put forward or at all. Most were, however, counselled in the best method of achieving their individual potential — sometimes through re-training or second-chance education. Today, they walk tall in newly-carved careers.

LISTENING — THE FOUNDATION OF SUCCESSFUL COUNSELLING

The essence of all successful human relationships is listening. When you are asked to listen and proceed to give advice, you are not doing what was asked. When asked to listen and you tell why the person should not feel the way they do, you trample on their feelings. When asked to listen and you rush to do something to solve the person's problems, you are failing them, strange as that may seem. Advice is cheap and most humans can do for themselves. They may be discouraged and faltering but people are generally not helpless. When you do for them what they can and need to do for themselves, you contribute to their fears and weakness.

This, first and foremost, must be the mindset of any successful counsellor. People who come for counselling are from diverse backgrounds and religious beliefs and, very often, no stated belief. Too often, they are the victims of indifference and intolerance. To benefit from counselling, they need to find compassion, a listening ear, a professional evaluation of prospects, an understanding of the difficulties experienced and guidance towards the best solution. Above all else, they need to feel respected as a human being, again part of the family of society.

The qualifications for this form of counselling are much broader than business assessment ability. That is, of course, an essential ingredient in counselling of the unemployed. However, it must be matched by genuine compassion, a capacity to avoid judgement based on personal morality or value systems, an ability to see behind the mask of despair or false bravado, to see the whole person and assess future potential. Very often, the person comes forward with an idea, however vague, which is his or her only lifeline to sanity. There is a high potential suicide risk. Rejection, however valid, can be the instrument which propels a fellow human into that ultimate despair. So one must tread softly, because you tread on dreams.

Of course, it would be unreasonable to encourage anyone to proceed with an idea or concept that is obviously doomed to failure. Properly structured counselling can focus a person's mind into potentially more rewarding channels. Most people who come for counselling have acquired scars, very often deep and raw from recent trauma. Like all human beings, their dearest wish is to be reborn without them. Although this cannot be done, if they have reasonable mental and physical health, virtually all can be helped to re-build lives.

The essential cornerstone of successful counselling is the art of listening. For this reason, I am grateful to the eminent Irish theologian and preacher, Fr. Eltin Griffin, OCarm. for his permission to use below material from a lecture, *Listening in the Gospels*:

> To really listen, there must be the capacity to hear through many wrappings, to listen beyond the outer layer of the word spoken. Words are often halting and many times plainly not what is meant. In any conversation involving two people there are six persons present. What each person said equals

two; what each person meant to say equals two; what each person understood the other to say equals two.

We have all acquired a whole host of attitudes which detrimentally affects our ability to listen.

- The first and most obvious usually applies more to teenagers and/or the immature person. This consists of bored inattention whilst we wait and wonder when the speaker will stop.
- More common is listening to classify what is being said. We then mentally label and file it into our own mental frame. Thereafter, we give the conversation only such attention as that frame calls for. We are no longer listening to a person but to a type.
- Then again, we listen with judgement on what is being revealed, comparing our own standards of values with the one who is speaking. Thus we effectively seal off any real understanding by us of the speaker.
- Far too often we listen, waiting to impose upon the speaker a detailed account of our own personal experiences. This blocks any real understanding or comprehension of what the speaker is trying to convey.
- Finally, we listen with a whole host of unconscious feelings which colour everything the speaker says. Our own unfaced fears, our own evaded decisions, our own deep-rooted prejudices, our own repressed longings and our own hidden aspirations.

So, with all of these unconscious feelings present within ourselves, the speaker is scarcely present even though he or she is giving out of the fullness of his or her ideas and feelings.

Now, if all of these deficiencies were heavily cloaked from the speaker, it would be one thing. However, nature itself provides the trap. Within each and every one of us, there exists a most sensitive "Spectator Listener" to our own speaking. This gives us a sharp awareness whether or not the person we are addressing is listening in depth to what we are saying. When this "Spectator Listener" recognises a defect in listening, it signals an immediate stop. Now the speaker withholds what he or she really feels, thinks and believes, simply because he/she is aware no one is really listening. A closure effect is created which waters down the expression of true feelings.

- To develop our true potential in human relationships, and particularly in counselling, we must develop the art of Agape or Open listening. The rules are few, simple and require only that we leap outside ourselves to:
- Listen with openness, acceptance and positive interest, an interest so alive that judgement is withheld.
- Listen with expectancy so as to evoke the fullest capacities of the speaker. Thus the person talking sees themselves in this new light of expectation. A listening patience, grounded in faith in what that person may become, can change that person's whole life.
- Listen with real involvement and understanding of the person's feelings, not merely his or her words. Listen as an AA listens to the alcoholic. Listen as a widow listens to a woman whose husband has just died. Listen as a priest will

listen to a colleague who is going through a crisis
of faith.

- Listen with care and concern. The person
  speaking must really matter to us as a fellow
  human being navigating the stormy seas of life.
  We must care enough to be involved even at
  some risk and real sacrifice to ourselves. We
  must remember that genuine, compassionate
  listening never, ever comes cheap.

To listen another person's heart and soul into a condition of
disclosure is probably the greatest service that any human being
can ever perform for another. That is why it is the central core to
successful counselling.

There is, however, a problem. Agape or open listening takes
time. In this new world of frenzied activity, we hoard time as a
miser hoards gold. We set aside limited time-spans to
accomplish specific tasks. It has been the experience of all who
have been successfully involved in counselling the unemployed
that no single counselling session can be governed by the clock.
It cannot be concluded until a new sense of purpose or hope
has been rekindled in the fellow human being who is the focus
of your attention. Trained counsellors, however, learn how to
develop individual techniques that enable them to seize the
correct moment for intervention which is the beginning of the
nurturing of new hope. It is the marriage of this
professionalism to the art of agape or open listening that
creates the richest harvest.

COUNSELLING — A NEED CREATED BY A MODERN WORLD

It is a tragedy of our modern world that we have all become so
self-centred. So long as our little corner of the universe makes
sense, we put the rest out of our minds.

Involuntary unemployment is not unlike being stricken with an illness. You are struck, you wilt and then you fight. You need to hold your standing place in the human race. The fight helps until you reach the day when you realise you can't win it — at least not without some outside help. The clock is running against you. You start plotting for some continuity. You invoke love and friendship, buying allies, making leagues and treaties. Then you are scared and sometimes desperate. You can only see darkness. Now you are dangerous because you are cornered. You are envious and resentful of the success of others. Then you become destructive, of others and yourself.

This is why the opening few moments of any counselling session are the most critical. A fumbling approach, a single false note, will arouse distrust or hostility. The counsellor must develop an overture that combines the right mixture of scientific detachment and professional interest.

The opening skilled manoeuvre requires both serene confidence and genuine empathy with the person being counselled. Just as disturbances deep in the earth can be recorded and observed with scientific interest, so also can disturbances of the soul and mind, which are usually discharged under the pressures of buried emotions. Just as a seismologist might watch a jagged graph reporting a fracture in the earth's crust, through careful observation and agape listening, the counsellor must assess the hopes and fears of the person who is being counselled.

An American colleague drew his inspiration from writer Morris West to define counselling:

> We are called to be mid-wives at the birth of a prodigy, a new beginning wrenched from the womb of previous individual and societal failure. Like all mid-wives we are summoned for our skills but can give no guarantees on what might be delivered, a stillbirth or a wonder child.

The language might be slightly overboard but I can understand where he came from. One of the very first counsellors at the coal-face after the racial riots in American cities, he went on to say:

> The profile of a counsellor is much the same as that of a good negotiator. The talents are much similar. Among these are a smiling countenance and an unshakeable composure. The composure must not be the white-knuckled restraint which betrays doubt, fear or anger. Doubt denotes incompetence, fear denotes a victim and anger an enemy. The composure needed is an attitude of total relaxation which says, more eloquently than words:
>
> *"We seek together truth, not contention; justice not advantage. We understand your difficulties and we are prepared to be patient."*

This is where the art of listening and the skill come in. You cannot work out the right smile by number. You must be able to reason yourself into it. The simplest reason, absolute interest and sincerity, is the best.

Counsellors must expect to deal with all sorts. Men and women, mature and immature, geniuses, idiots and sociopaths — you name them, you get them. During counselling sessions after the racial riots in the US, many counsellors faced a knife or a gun simply because of some perceived false note or phrase. Gentling down the angry person became a very necessary life-skill.

A number of fairly common attitude errors emerge during role-playing in training:

- Some, mistakenly, develop a technique of putting themselves in command from the first moment. This is a mistake that can lead to ever greater mistakes

- Others try to unsettle the person being interviewed first and then gentle them down. This will very likely lead to a conflict situation within the recipient

- Others regard early counselling as a challenge to their own professional status, which they are forced to confront. This replaces agape listening with a hasty rush to judgement. The most painful aspect of coming for counselling for most people is when, in their fragility, they are forced to open themselves to a stranger. Very often you are dealing with a damaged person, tortured by the inner guilt of failure although, for all that fragility, there can be cold calculation based on winning approval. A forced pacing triggers this into action.

Some who come for counselling have reached that solitary road where even the stranger passing the time of day is a fortunate encounter. Here sincere and genuine empathy is the only hope of opening up the heart and soul to revelation.

Others try to hide from the counsellor a host of emotions with an overpowering character, trying to control the interview. Here, calm cool reaction is essential and the avoidance of too early intervention into the conversation.

It is critical to remember that most people who come for counselling have reached that moment in a crisis when reality slides out of focus. They live precariously but passionately in a dimension of dreaming. They are people in flight — from the past, from a threatening future, from a self that is incomplete and out of balance. They seek an impossible newness. To create it, they become myth-makers.

The problem the counsellor will always face is to distinguish between the poetic truth and the actual. One must always remember that what is left unsaid is sometimes more important than what is expressed, however vivid and persuasive the words. Because every concealment and half-truth can erode a fragment of the relationship you try to build, a rush to judgement is fatal. Bluntness can shatter the illusion.

It is dangerous to make somebody question everything they did, said or even believed. It is very difficult for any of us to see ourselves in plain focus. We all have secrets from ourselves, otherwise we could not bear to live with ourselves.

All the time we come back to agape or open listening. Learn not to push, lead the person along their own road to a decision. That said, no two people are similar. No two counsellors will be comfortable with the same approach. To try and determine a single, stereotyped manner for counselling would be both wrong and self-defeating. Each counsellor must develop their own individual techniques and strengths.

Central to unemployment counselling is the proven fact that there is a very significant percentage of persons who are suicide risks. In my own experience, borne out by that of colleagues, this can be as high as 10% in any one year. There were two actual suicides on programmes in which I participated; I shared with colleagues the deep soul-searching that followed these tragic events.

To avoid any misunderstanding, let us be very clear. Potential suicide amongst the unemployed is not a normal or regular event. One can certainly counsel for weeks or months without encountering a single instance of a person at risk. But because the numbers are still statistically significant, it is essential for the counsellor to be aware and to be on guard. How are counsellors able to detect the person who falls into this category?

The clearest explanation is that, in life, we all experience pain, fear, injustice, confusion and death. We struggle to stay whole during the experience. Even in failure, we try to salvage ourselves from the wreckage. To some, however, the experience of failure is intolerable. They lose faith in God and man. They reach a point of despair where their very personality is fragmented. They suffer a loss of identity. Reason rocks under a barrage of contradictions. The will is frozen in a syncope of impotence. In this state, they are likely to contemplate suicide unless they are helped.

Initially, in such cases, you must spend time — a lot of time — and effort to create a condition of self-recognition, a condition in which even the confusion makes sense. Then you try to rebuild a sense of self-belief and hope for the future. The person before you is a fellow human being in distress and not merely a statistic.

The simple fact of need creates the imperative to action to relieve a brother or sister's pain.

If we can guide a person to look behind the artefacts of life to the Divinity that they conceal, then loneliness and despair will disappear. The same Spirit is immanent everywhere. Unless we have a perception of unity, the world becomes an unbearable chaos with no present meaning and no hope of future restoration. The greatest good that any counsellor can achieve is to urge the person before them outwards in growth. Service, love, the simplest interest in the world can be a step towards personal achievement and the source of all happiness.

One fact is clear to me after nearly 30 years of counselling. A great number of us live in plastic capsules, wanting but not daring to get out. We become prisoners of our genes, our history and of our ancestral ambitions and dreams. We try to escape our past and shut it out behind a plastic wall. Only when we learn to confront it can we come to terms with its true meaning.

All persons who undertake counselling need to have within themselves the serenity of faith and belief. Only then is it possible to listen with openness, acceptance and positive interest, to listen without judgement and with expectancy so as to evoke the fullest capacity of the person before us.

As will be clear from previous analysis, this will bring the person before us to see themselves in a new light of expectation. Our own listening patience, grounded in our own serenity of belief and faith in what the person may become, can change that person's whole life.

The true fruits of faith are completeness and total harmony. If we ourselves have faith in God and reliance on His all powerful Spirit within us, we can navigate the person before us through even severe crisis. It is this which, coupled with agape listening and careful mental analysis, enables us to discover a goal which can be aimed at and to clearly recognise that goal as attainable. Because, as counsellors, our minds are uncluttered by the difficulties being experienced by the person before us, we are usually first to reach that point of discovery. Now the important thing is to forget the time element altogether. Otherwise, we rush ourselves into hasty decision-making. The work is more important than what is produced, the journey more important than the arrival. This is the art of living that we have forgotten in this mechanical world of ours. If we rediscover, we find we can accomplish and help others accomplish sometimes far beyond our dreams.

Section 3

APPLYING THE PRINCIPLES IN A TIGER ECONOMY

Through the example of current community enterprise projects, this section explains how the principles of community enterprise, as set out in the previous section, can be applied in practice. In the final chapter, the author sets out his vision for a new Ireland.

Chapter 10

A LIMERICK COMMUNITY RESPONSE

It is part of the human psyche to assume that disasters will happen to others but never to ourselves. Perhaps this is a necessary life-skill. Blessed the hand that weaves the veil which hides the future.

Over the years, throughout the western world, I have seen communities devastated by plant closures. The fear, disbelief and pinched spirits of the victim people is a poignant, enduring memory.

In April 1999, this was the trauma that faced the communities of Southill in Limerick. For over 30 years, the Krups plant had been the main employer in the area, employing over 800 people at its peak in 1998. But, in April 1999, the plant was permanently closed with the direct loss of the remaining 500 jobs and the potential loss of a further 700 jobs in related services.

The government set up an inter-agency task force with a view to marketing the site and seeking a replacement industry. None was found. The size of the property — a 16-acre site and 164,000 square feet of buildings together with 11 houses — made it unlikely that a single replacement industry could be found in any reasonable timeframe. If the site were sold on the open market, its strategic location made it a likely site for a retail park development with a very much lower employment quotient.

As the weeks grew into months, the empty plant stood as a stark monument to the collapse of the local community economy.

Located on the periphery of Limerick city, in the middle of a densely-populated area consisting of nearly 12,000 people, the plant was within walking distance of the former employees. Southill quickly became the most disadvantaged area of Limerick city. Unemployment exceeded 40% of the adult population, bringing all the consequential deprivation — welfare dependency, poverty and economic marginalisation. The socio-economic profile was akin to that of the West Tallaght communities before the SVP and other similar programmes began to impact.

Then a new dynamic entered the equation, turning the tide of disaster into success. Spearheaded initially by the Limerick Enterprise Network in close collaboration with Paul Partnership, meetings were held involving Limerick Corporation, Shannon Development, IBEC, the Limerick Diocesan authorities and Limerick County Council. From these meetings developed a bold and imaginative proposal — a company would be formed, Limerick Enterprise Development Partnership Limited (LEDP), which would acquire the whole site from the owners, Group Moulinex, for IR£2.75 million. The purchase was concluded in November 1999.

LEDP is a company limited by guarantee and set up for purely charitable purposes. All profits from its activities must be devoted to the charitable purposes for which it was formed. The company is precluded by law from distributing any part of the profits to its members. Being a genuine partnership of the private sector, State agencies and local organisations, including the Diocese of Limerick and local authorities, the company derived its funding from a mixture of private, public and EU sources, with the initial seven investors each contributing £150,000.

LEDP sought the best professional advice available. From the very beginning, it was recognised that bricks and mortar alone would not provide the magic ingredient for social revitalisation and job creation. It was decided to convert the entire premises into an Enterprise Centre. The former Operations Manager of

Krups was engaged as Project Director and General Manager. IIis intimate knowledge of the facility, of the ethos of the founders of LEDP and his extensive business network would, it was felt, ensure successful development.

Initial research demonstrated that, within a very short timeframe, a sufficient number of tenants could be attracted from the wider South-West region to make the Enterprise Centre a viable, economic enterprise. However, since the majority of such tenants, which were successful businesses, would bring with them an existing workforce, this would have only a marginal impact on the unemployment and disadvantage of the people of Southill.

Although, at the time of writing, this project is still in its early embryonic stage, the promoters are anxious to avoid the pitfall of LEDP being perceived as the "grand provider", promoting a dependency culture that is the greatest barrier to community innovation, enterprise and entrepreneurship.

A meeting of the pastoral teams serving these communities was organised by the Diocese of Limerick. Chaired by the Chief Executive of Paul Partnership, the LEDP proposals were outlined and the meeting heard of how the success achieved by SVP in Tallaght had come about.

It is hoped that, with the encouragement of both the Diocese and Paul Partnership, a suitable community-based grouping will emerge that can emulate the success achieved by the communities in Tallaght.

It was recognised that counselling of the specialist nature described in **Chapter 9** had been a major contributory factor in the success achieved by SVP in Tallaght. The lessons from that programme provided a solid basis for similar success in a Limerick programme that remained "A Limerick solution to a Limerick problem".

Paul Partnership and the Limerick Diocese hope in the early future to source, from the broader Limerick region, people who have the interest and broad ability to undertake counselling. It is recognised that this may not be achievable in any short timeframe. However, when a sufficiently strong grouping is identified, seminar training can be organised so that the interest and ability can be honed and sharpened to the fullest extent required to undertake effective counselling. If achieved, this will be the first time ever in Ireland that this training was made an integral part of a partnership response to community deprivation and unemployment.

The Directors of LEDP are well aware that there were very strong Limerick Associations in the US, with members who had attained high business and professional standing. They are also aware that a significant number of emigrants from the Limerick area have succeeded in the US in developing innovative technologies and products. They are very conscious of the Israeli precedent of using the skills of the Diaspora to build or rebuild local economies. It is felt that, when the Enterprise Centre on the former Krups site is fully developed and operational, this could provide the incentive to set up a Trust Fund to which subscriptions would be invited from the US.

The primary objective of this Trust Fund, if or when established, would be to assist Limerick and Limerick region emigrants, who had sound business ideas, to repatriate to their homeland. The intention would be to use this resource to establish businesses in those areas of the Limerick region requiring new innovative manufacturing and/or service ideas to kick-start the revitalisation of the local community economy. Such a Trust could have wide powers to give general assistance by way of grant or soft loans to assist the development of social regeneration and jobs in the region. The organisation of such a Trust would be a mammoth task; achieving maximum success in the development of the Enterprise Centre would provide a focus and incentive to undertake this effort.

To the best of my knowledge, this is the first time ever that the full complement of US community revitalisation planning has been introduced anywhere in Europe. The Limerick programme has the potential to attain the same measure of success as comparable US programmes. It demonstrates the relevance of community empowerment and community partnership to a whole range of problems which, in either a greater or lesser way, affects other EU communities.

The membership of LEDP has a huge significance for other areas of Ireland and Europe. The interaction between the private enterprise-developed Limerick Enterprise Network, the Diocese of Limerick, the Paul Partnership, the local authorities and State agencies is an event of special significance.

The role of Paul Partnership demonstrates that at least one of the local partnerships set up under the 1991 PESP has adopted in full measure the real objective and intent of such partnerships. The fact that Paul Partnership has a former government minister as Chairman and a Chief Executive recruited from the private sector may explain its willingness to accept innovation over precedent.

The leadership provided by the Limerick Enterprise Network shows that private enterprise in Limerick is motivated by a strong social conscience and a willingness of executives to apply their individual skills, without reward, to the less fortunate within society.

The role of the Diocesan Authorities points the way to a missionary method of great importance — the reintroduction of the Church into private and public life through works of practical charity. Historically, this method has been the beginning of the most permanent evangelical activity.

The willingness of Shannon Development to participate actively shows that some at least of the spirit of Brendan O'Regan, the founder of SFADCO, remains alive and well in that organisation. He was one of the earliest exponents of the credo that the solution to unemployment and social deprivation would not come from the State agencies, but would have to be worked out in and by communities.

The participation of the Limerick Corporation and Limerick County Council demonstrates that Irish local authorities have every ounce of the same public service willingness as their UK counterparts. It also begs the question as to when central government is prepared to remove the restraints on this vital local asset.

The membership of LEDP will actively encourage all of the educational establishments in Limerick city and county to become involved; this is a pointer to a much wider form of social partnership that can truly address social exclusion and the educational deficit which it highlights.

The wide vision that LEDP has adopted for its mission commands the attention and support of all of the people of Limerick who aspire to see the potential of that city fully realised. Such a bold and imaginative approach is the surest foundation for ultimate and outstanding success.

For these reasons, it is very possible that this Limerick programme will provide the beacon of hope when storm clouds impact other Irish or EU communities.

Chapter 11

BUILDING A PERMANENT AND DURABLE TIGER SOCIETY — A NEW VISION OF IRISH SOCIETY

There has been a huge volume of spoken and written criticism in recent years of the Irish corporate sector — the revelations emerging from public enquiries over the past three years have done very little to assuage public perception of untrammelled corporate greed. Of course, virtually all companies have a list of charities to which cash donations are made; without this, very many of our excellent charities would have inadequate resources to meet the demands of those they serve.

Although cynics may dismiss corporate charitable giving as mere public relations, it is worthwhile, in the context of our analysis of the present Tiger economy, to focus on examples of genuine corporate care and compassion for the by-passed in our society.

Vision Consulting Limited is a Dublin-based company, founded in 1984, that has expanded internationally. It now has offices in Belfast, Edinburgh, London and New York, with six internationally-known names as strategic partners. A private company, Vision is a business change and information technology consultancy with annual revenues in excess of IR£20 million. Its services are sought by some of the leading international banking and investment groups. Its Chief Executive has always believed that societal difficulties can not be solved merely by throwing money at the problems. For this reason, and for many years, he has made available to several leading Irish charities both monetary and human resources of his company — yet he always ensured that the public relations was focused on the charity and not on his company.

Recently, this work has been expanded by the formation of a charitable trust, Vision Trust Limited, which has already undertaken a direct role in providing skills training to many of the less fortunate youth of our society. The trust also makes available, on a voluntary basis, the full range of professional skills within Vision Consulting to community groups and self-help projects.

This is the kind of corporate social compassion and responsibility that can help eliminate the sharp divisions the Celtic Tiger has created within our Irish society.

The private enterprise companies that are a significant part of the LEDP charitable company also illustrate a similar social consciousness. It would have been a financial coup for them to have acquired the former Krups premises and land for a variety of developments with a very much lower employment quotient. Instead, they took a decision to invest time and monetary resources, in a unique public/private sector charitable partnership, to ensure community benefit.

The Limerick programme is also an excellent example of how a community, devastated by plant closure, can be organised to respond and turn disaster into success. Even the most optimistic of our Celtic Tiger advocates will accept that inevitably there will be other closures, and other communities stricken with fear and disbelief. They need the lessons of Tallaght and Limerick in their time of need, as do also the other areas of Ireland which today, like Southill, are by-passed by the Celtic Tiger. As already stated, the whole programme can be adapted to restore vitality to our dying villages and towns, big or small, rebuilding community and the local economy.

However, there is an imperative for the whole people of Ireland today to address one simple, pregnant question. What type of society do we want for the 21st century?

Over 50 years ago, economics journalist Arnold Marsh published his vision of Irish society in the *Irish Review*. In his thesis, March argued that, instead of attempting to develop in isolation to communities, there was an urgent need for more co-operative development along the lines of the Finnish and Scandinavian models. He saw the local co-operative society as "a centre of help, education and social and business life", a definition that might equally be applied to the modern community enterprise initiative.

Marsh argued that the State should give a lead in developing Irish resources, on a community by community basis. The list of areas that he pinpointed makes fascinating reading today. He called for a programme of afforestation, the conversion of sewage into fertiliser and methane gas and the provision of hatcheries for fresh water fisheries development. He wanted to utilise wind energy, either to pump water to high-level reservoirs for the general supply of electricity or for the production by electrolysis of hydrogen as a source of motive power. He pointed to the resources that we might cull from the sea by extracting minerals like magnesium, copper, iodine and bromide from seaweed. He called for the exploration and development of our land-based mineral resources and the use of turf as a raw material for the chemical industry. To grow warm-climate and out-of-season fruit and vegetables, he urged that the use of glasshouse growing should be greatly extended. And, pointing to the need to conserve resources, he insisted we should regulate water levels instead of draining land haphazardly by gravity alone, and increase the storage capacity of the Shannon system by means of embankment and pumping - a proposal that, 50 years later, might find a welcoming echo in the hearts of the owners of many a flooded farmland!

Marsh argued against building our industrial economy on foreign investment, except where that had special advantage, since "depending on them would only make us helpless in times of general trade depression". Instead, he called on government to provide capital loans at attractive terms to encourage native entrepreneurs and to introduce tax reliefs on profits re-invested in business. As for the State, he argued it could, and should, embark on enterprises that would bring prosperity to the nation, even though they might not at first have any prospects of making direct profits. It should do so on a large enough scale to provide adequate employment in local communities. The list of promising projects of this kind was, he stated, long but embarking on them on as large a scale as was feasible would bring prosperity and contentment at once, together with a great increase in our national resources.

Marsh admitted that the programme he proposed would cost over £500 million but argued that we could not stem emigration and the erosion of young people from our communities "if we demanded direct dividends from every item of national investment".

Marsh was writing at a time when the concept of self-sufficiency was still alive and more than 10 years before the First Programme for Economic Expansion. There is little evidence that his words were taken seriously.

The late Dr. David Thornley, Associate Professor of Political Science at Trinity College, reflected the more widely held view of Irish economic potential when he wrote, in 1970:

> Two basic factors, one economic and one geographic, have for long cast their shadow over the politics of Ireland. The first is that the island possesses no abundance of mineral resources and, consequently, no tradition of industrial development. This means that Ireland has been dependent for its national wealth upon agricultural production and upon importation for the bulk of the artefacts that sustain industrial civilisation. Today and for the foreseeable future, Ireland is, therefore, defined by economic circumstances as essentially an

exporter of primary agricultural produce, notably cattle, and an importer of heavy industrial equipment and consumer goods. For these reasons the Irish people have for centuries been condemned to the proportionately low standard of living that is often the concomitant of agricultural production; it has also made Irish economics, and therefore Irish politics, abnormally sensitive to external forces over which the political state of Ireland can have no control.

This description mirrors the view of Ireland that was held by administrators prior to independence and adopted, seemingly without question, by successive governments since then. It is my conviction that this vision, if vision it can be called, is based on an assessment which was and is largely untested. If we had carried out an open-minded analysis of the strengths and weaknesses of the nation, we would have discovered the potential of our resources long ago. This potential would have provided the only sound basis on which to develop the economy.

Work has been carried out to some extent in the exploration of natural gas, lead and zinc but, at best, it is undertaken only in a piecemeal fashion. Even today, the potential of the seas around us remains a mystery. A representative of the Irish Geological Survey Office is on record as saying:

> 90% of what we now know about the seabed around our coast has been learned in the past 30 years or so. What we don't know would still fill volumes.

And so, instead of facing the challenge of creating our own unique, national vision of a future Ireland, we are drifting into a dependency on European hand-outs and an industrial policy driven by attracting multi-nationals to establish in Ireland.

We have already touched on the fact that the Programmes for Economic Expansion of the late 1950s and early 1960s virtually abandoned Irish-owned businesses in favour of attracting the multi-nationals to Ireland, with generous grants and tax concessions not available to the existing Irish companies. This could, perhaps, be defended on the grounds of cold economics — it was the least expensive method of developing a largely-agricultural into an industrial economy. But it virtually ignored important sociological factors and ethics. It gave rise to the massive migration/emigration from rural areas of our country. More and more people were forced, by economic necessity, to live in the concrete jungles that are our cities.

In 1999, there were 40,000 plus applicants seeking local authority housing, mainly in city and urban areas. Thus, in this new Camelot, there are huge numbers living in sub-standard accommodation or relying on the charity of family and friends for shelter, often in overcrowded conditions. Indeed, in an RTE *Prime Time* discussion in February 2000, a Labour Party survey was quoted which indicated that, nationally, there were 160,000 plus persons seeking housing who were unable to afford the present cost.

The number of homeless was estimated by the State in March 1999 at 5,000. Several organisations, directly involved, regarded this as a gross underestimate. The Chief Executive of one such organisation estimated the figure in December 1999 at 10,000 plus. He was convinced of his facts but feared to be the source of the information as his organisation was dependent in part on State grants; politicians were reluctant to have such a blot on the Tiger economy highlighted!

In turn, this has led to a situation where, at Christmas 1999, there were thousands of homeless people, hungry and without hope and very many potentially suicidal. The papers over that Christmas period pinpointed the lonely deaths of two — from malnutrition, cold and despair. Not only was there no room at the inn, there was no room even in the shelters for the homeless! How many of us saw the living Christ in these poor sick failures, as we went about Christmas preparations? In the inhuman, impersonal cities that have replaced nuclear communities, the cult of the individual has become dominant. We are afraid of the consequences of getting involved. Meanwhile, the rural communities where, in my experience, caring for the old, the infirm and the poor was part of life's ethic are decimated. Holiday homes and transient holiday populations, supported by generous tax concessions, have replaced what were vibrant, living communities.

It need not be so. Study any business directory and you could identify thousands of businesses, large and small, that could operate with equal, and perhaps better, efficiency in a nuclear rural community. In fact, the whole development of the Internet and the growth of sales on that medium makes location far less important than the past. I know several computer programmers who work from their homes in rural areas and supply to software companies in the UK and even the US.

The future of any community depends on all of its people. This is particularly true of our younger generation. The future is bleak indeed if we continue to permit, and indeed encourage, the haemorrhage of our young, particularly those who have acquired education and skills, to dream only of migration to the cities or emigration as the sole hope of a reasonable livelihood. Remember, whether people are disadvantaged or privileged, handicapped or gifted, it is the sum total of their dreams that equates the reality of tomorrow.

Every Christmas, in churches of all denominations in the cities, towns, villages and rural areas of Ireland, congregations swell as preachers welcome home our emigrants. There is a feel-good factor as families and communities are reunited that heightens the sadness of the inevitable parting.

There is a saying amongst the desert nomad of the Middle East, "Never wave good-bye to the caravan, you will follow it soon". This is often so, so true of the younger members of families growing up in a community that offers no prospects. Then, all too soon, the death of parents sees the demise, too, of the light in the window and the welcome at the door. What were vibrant family year-around dwellings are sold as holiday homes to European or Irish buyers, as a careful study of the rural property market over the past three years demonstrates. Staying away becomes almost inevitable; although, as one emigrant poet, Fr. John O'Connor in his poem *The Call of Home* wrote, "Lord, the home Thou gavest once, could they forget?". The erosion of the young creates ghost communities. This is the human face of our failure, if we neglect to empower ourselves to revitalise our own community.

It is possible, by ignoring the social consequences, to raise an economic argument in favour of abandoning the Midlands, the South-West, West and North-West. By concentrating all development along the eastern seaboard, the rest can be allowed to become a vast national park!

Farming, even small farming, is a seven days a week, 52 weeks of the year job. If, as is predicted, most of the Irish farms become uneconomic and are incapable of providing an adequate living to the operators, without the availability of other part-time employment, the erosion of youth will toll the death-knell of the family farm. Part-time employment can only be provided by industry and business located within the communities. When city dwellers go into the countryside to enjoy the pastoral scene and peace, they need to remember that this is preserved by the blood, sweat and tears of farmers who work for long hours, in all kinds of weather, to keep the countryside intact. Without that labour, most of the farmland would revert to a form of natural jungle.

Already, there is a dangerous imbalance between countryside and concrete jungle on the Irish East coast. Unless urgent, remedial action is taken now, we risk the danger of our green and fertile island being lost to future generations. We have, within the existing Tiger economy, the resources to turn the tide. To do so will require a new alliance of the Irish people — an alliance to communities nation-wide, to restore community values, to recapture control over our local community economies, to develop employment opportunities for our people in the location of their choice and, above all else, to establish a national vision that will preserve this green and verdant land in perpetuity for our children and our children's children. Since such a vision would embody the principle of cherishing all of the children of the nation equally, it is surely a vision to which social partners including farming bodies, co-operatives, credit unions and trade unions can enthusiastically subscribe? It will not come about by chance. The charade of politically formulated regional authorities or the mythology of decentralisation of government offices will do little to assist. It can only be built, brick by brick, community by community, by the combined will and determination of the people.

Politicians have already demonstrated their inability to adopt such a vision. Eighty years after independence they are obliged to admit that people have grown disillusioned with politics, do not trust politicians and have little faith in any of the political parties. Perhaps, the people of Ireland, by banding together in the strength of community, can also bring about a much-needed transformation of Irish political life.

We are all familiar with the much-publicised stories of great works of art discovered after lying for decades, unrecognised and unacknowledged, in a variety of institutions and schools throughout Britain and Ireland. The Caravaggio, donated some years ago by the Irish Jesuits to the National Gallery of Ireland, is one excellent example. This illustrates how successive generations of those in control of the worldly assets of these institutions have a penchant for accepting, without question, the inventory and value of their predecessors of these items. This unquestioning acceptance of things as they are is rampant in communities all over the globe. It is the single most important barrier faced by communities seeking to claim control over their own destinies.

Few communities posses a Caravaggio, though virtually all have assets of people and resources that can dramatically impact their local economies. The people of Southill in Limerick saw only a closed factory. More observant minds saw the means of rejuvenating the local economy.

One of the Tallaght community groups met in a hall of a local community school, sited on a small hill and commanding an excellent view of the whole surrounding area. The Dublin mountains were in the background and, from this vantage point, the group had a clear view of several roads. When, during discussion, the facilitator probed where these roads went, it was discovered there was a wealth of historical sites, woodlands filled with flower, fauna and wildlife, three ancient castles and one former monastic site — all within a radius of between 10 and 20 miles. Members of the group gradually remembered seeing walking, bird-watching and cycling groups as well as scout troops using this location as the springboard for day trips of discovery. Was this an asset with potential?

With the aid of a grant from the local Enterprise Board, a survey of the area's potential for tourism, school trips, special interest groups exploration and/or visitor day bus trips was undertaken. The six-month research project proved very rewarding. Its report produced formed the basis for a co-operative effort that provided buses collecting from visitors to Dublin from hotels, school children and a range of ladies' clubs and active retired groups for day-long trips. These provided a pleasant recreation for the participants and year-round jobs for a group of previously unemployed people.

Over how many years had this same group looked out on this landscape and seen only a scenic backdrop?

It is wise to remember that the previously rejected can be the cornerstone of a community area's recovery. People can live and work in a district for upwards of 30 years and still fail to identify the physical assets or potential assets of their own townland.

I remember, during a stroll one evening in the west of Ireland after delivering a lecture, meeting an eminent botanist. He had stopped on a car journey because a colleague had previously spotted a particularly rare species of plant. He told me how its presence pointed to the suitability of the soil for the growth of a wide range of plants and flowers.

Subsequent community enquiry revealed this had a very sizeable commercial potential. Yet, the land in question had lain fallow for over a decade.

On another occasion, in northern England, there was a rat-infested old mill which was locally regarded as an eyesore, a liability to the area. When an audit of the area's potential revealed the existence of several natural pure wells on the adjoining grounds, the local community partnership group acquired the site at a modest cost. Their intention was to demolish the mill in favour of a more modern structure. A retired architect persuaded the group to refurbish it.

Today, the mill building houses a food-processing business, drawing its water requirements from the wells and its power from a restructured mill race.

In yet another area of the UK, a much-despised old branch railway shed provided the focal point for a

newly-developed private rail system, intended as a
tourist attraction. The provision of the railway
helped the local group to re-establish a unique fire
brick manufacture from local clay, some 70 years
after a similar project operating in the area had
closed.

The list is endless. Mines that were closed have been reopened as
tourist attractions; old buildings as heritage centres; slag heaps as
the raw material for innovative decorative garden bricks and
walls; abandoned buildings redesigned as people centres
providing a diverse range of services to meet local needs.

It is gratifying to see how, in so many cases, community
stewardship of a multitude of different sites, protect wildlife and
flora and enable the community to have a direct role in
environmental protection and planning.

Recent social surveys have demonstrated that a significant
number of today's farmers anticipate that farming of the future
will, at best, be a part-time occupation, uneconomic without
other paid employment. In most parts of rural Ireland, such
employment can only be generated by the form of community
initiative we have discussed.

This apart, I worked in the US when factory farming took a
dominant role in the US agricultural industry. Factory farming is
very largely machinery-intensive. I witnessed community groups
of small farmers coming together in an endeavour to preserve
their way of life and try to reverse the tide. They co-operated to
produce a vast range of organic foods and vegetables, which,
unlike factory farming, was and is labour-intensive. They
developed to supply their produce — sometimes by air — to
locations hundreds and thousands of miles away where they
brought a premium price from discerning buyers. Ireland has a
green image. Why not use this to grow organic food for the
markets of Europe? Why not do, as US small farmers did,
package and blast-freeze for a year around market?

Were these US or any of the other communities referred to in earlier chapters more intelligent or more advantaged than your own. They were not. They all started with a small group of people looking at a common measure of societal deprivation that they sought to alleviate. Instead of reinventing the wheel, they learned from the success of others.

It all comes down to that famous phrase of George Bernard Shaw, made immortal in more recent times by the Kennedy brothers:

> Some see things as they are and ask WHY?
> I dream things as they never were and ask WHY NOT?